PRAISE FOR *THE GOD OF NEW BEGINNINGS*

"The more I'm around the Genesis Project guys, the more impressed I am with how they're applying the love and grace of Christ to salvage messed-up people (the kind whose worried relatives and friends call my daily radio program, *New Life Live!*, every day). I've even made the effort to travel to see this work in action. It ties directly into a heart concern of mine, which is transforming lives through God's truth in redemptive relationships."

—STEPHEN ARTERBURN, NEW LIFE MINISTRIES
FOUNDER AND CHAIRMAN

"Raw, gritty, practical, and inspirational, this is essential reading for anyone with a passion to bring the beautiful news to the broken. Highly recommended!"

—JEFF LUCAS, INTERNATIONAL AUTHOR,
SPEAKER, BROADCASTER

"*The God of New Beginnings* is a piercing documentary of desperate people in desperate places who are transformed by Jesus Christ. Nothing is held back. It builds on story after story, truth after truth, faith to faith, and glory to glory. What Rob and Matt show us is raw and real. It took my breath away and challenged me to believe each day for more of God's power in my own life!"

—RICHARD FOTH, SPEAKER AND AUTHOR, *KNOWN*

The
GOD
of NEW
BEGINNINGS

The
GOD
of NEW
BEGINNINGS

How the Power of Relationship
Brings Hope and Redeems Lives

ROB COWLES AND MATT ROBERTS

WITH DEAN MERRILL

W Publishing Group

An Imprint of Thomas Nelson

Published in Nashville, Tennessee, by W Publishing, an imprint of Thomas Nelson.

Published in association with the literary agency of Wolgemuth & Associates, Inc.

Thomas Nelson titles may be purchased in bulk for educational, business, fund-raising, or sales promotional use. For information, please e-mail SpecialMarkets@ThomasNelson.com.

Unless otherwise noted, Scripture quotations are taken from the Holy Bible, New International Version®, NIV®. © 1973, 1978, 1984, 2011 by Biblica, Inc.® Used by permission of Zondervan. All rights reserved worldwide.

Scripture quotations marked KJV are from the King James Version. Public domain.

Scripture quotations marked THE MESSAGE are from *The Message*. © by Eugene H. Peterson 1993, 1994, 1995, 1996, 2000, 2001, 2002. Used by permission of NavPress. All rights reserved. Represented by Tyndale House Publishers, Inc.

Scripture quotations marked NKJV are from the New King James Version®. © 1982 by Thomas Nelson. Used by permission. All rights reserved.

Scripture quotations marked NLV are from the New Life Version. © Christian Literature International.

Scripture quotations marked NLT are from the Holy Bible, New Living Translation. © 1996, 2004, 2007, 2013, 2015 by Tyndale House Foundation. Used by permission of Tyndale House Publishers, Inc., Carol Stream, Illinois 60188. All rights reserved.

Any Internet addresses, phone numbers, or company or product information printed in this book are offered as a resource and are not intended in any way to be or to imply an endorsement by Thomas Nelson, nor does Thomas Nelson vouch for the existence, content, or services of these sites, phone numbers, companies, or products beyond the life of this book.

ISBN 978-0-7852-2042-8 (eBook)

Library of Congress Cataloging-in-Publication Data

Names: Cowles, Rob, 1965- author. | Roberts, Matt, 1978- author. | Merrill, Dean, author.
Title: The God of new beginnings : how the power of relationship brings hope and redeems lives / Rob Cowles and Matt Roberts with Dean Merrill.
Description: Nashville, Tennessee : W Publishing, an imprint of Thomas Nelson, [2018]
Identifiers: LCCN 2018022540| ISBN 9780785220350 | ISBN 9780785220428 (eBook)
Subjects: LCSH: Non-church-affiliated people. | Evangelistic work.
Classification: LCC BV4921.3 .C69 2018 | DDC 248.4—dc23 LC record available at https://lccn.loc.gov/2018022540

Printed in the United States of America

18 19 20 21 22 LSC 6 5 4 3 2 1

CONTENTS

CONTENTS

PART ONE

A GOD
FOR MESSY
PEOPLE

I

"ANYBODY WANNA BUY A STRIP CLUB?"

If you follow the various best-places-to-live-in-America rankings, you would not imagine that a city as classy, beautiful, and educated as Fort Collins, Colorado, would even have a strip club. Nestled up against the majestic Rocky Mountains, with world-class ski slopes less than two hours away, its 160,000 residents enjoy more than 300 days of sunshine a year. Biking trails are everywhere, much to the delight of the 33,000 students at Colorado State University, the city's intellectual anchor.

My family and I have enjoyed the Fort Collins culture ever since 2005, when I (Rob) became executive pastor of Timberline Church, the city's largest, with more than five thousand attenders and a beautiful, expansive campus. I loved the opportunity to speak in the midweek services (as well as some weekends) while also managing a staff of a hundred. My wife, Joy, was a devoted mom to our two sons, the younger of whom was still in junior high, coming up through an excellent school system. We hardly noticed the seedy industrial area on the northeast side of town called the Mulberry Corridor (along Mulberry Street) near Interstate 25.

One day in the spring of 2013, I got a text from our senior pastor, Dary Northrop. He mentioned a guy named Aaron, who had come around saying he had given his life to Jesus and wanted to get out of the strip club business he and his two brothers had inherited from their father. Aaron Bekkela called again and is asking me to come over and at least see the property, Dary wrote. I agreed to meet him there tomorrow afternoon. Want to come with me? I texted back a yes, not really knowing what I was getting myself into. I had never been to a strip club before, and the only time I had even passed by the Hunt Club was when I was dropping off my kids at the curiously placed roller-skating rink next door.

The next day after lunch, the two of us plus another staff pastor made our way to the establishment. There we saw a nondescript, low-slung building with a small parking lot and a dingy sign out front that read

Hunt Club—GIRLS—GIRLS. Open Daily @ 4:00 pm. Open Friday @ Noon.

Up and down the block were various auto repair shops, a heating and plumbing contractor, and a tattoo parlor; directly behind the club was a trailer park.

Aaron, a fortyish man with red hair and a goatee, was waiting in his standard jeans and T-shirt to meet us. His personal story, I found out later, was no charade; he had been affected years before by a brief conversation one night at the end of a shift when one of his dancers had stopped by his office before leaving. Hanging around the door frame, she said, "Um, my mother asked me to give you a message."

Aaron had braced himself. Hearing from a dancer's mother could never go well, he assumed. But to his great surprise, the dancer had meekly said, "She just said to tell you, she and her friends [who happened to be Timberline women] are praying for you." This was a seed that would germinate in Aaron's life for years.

More recently, a random flyer had shown up in his mailbox promoting a Christian conference. He decided to go and ended up making a commitment to Jesus at that conference. His new life as a Christ follower prodded him to try to convince his two brothers that they should sell. He was tired of living with the tension of doing a men's Bible study in the morning and opening the club at night. He had approached several northern Colorado churches to step up and repurpose the property. He was desperate to extricate himself from this wretched livelihood. Maybe this building could even be redeemed for something positive.

One after another, the various pastors had replied, "That's an intriguing idea, and I commend you for living out your new faith in this way. But I have no idea what my church would do with a strip club!"

When he felt like there was nowhere else to turn, Aaron and his brothers tried to sell the business to another club in Denver, an hour away. In fact, they had landed a contract, but just before closing the deal, the buyer backed out with no explanation.

Now he had come knocking on Timberline's door once again.

The Perfume of Brokenness

We followed Aaron into the dimly lit building, which was entirely quiet at that hour of the day. Immediately I noticed how utterly dirty it was. No broom, vacuum cleaner, or dustcloth had been used there in a long, long time. Just inside the front door was a small office, and then a bar stretching along one wall. A vending machine on the left offered an array of candy bars, soda, cigarettes—and panties!

A coatrack with old, dirty housecoat-style robes caught by eye. What were those for? I found out later that when the scantily clad girls would go outside in the winter for a smoke, they'd just throw on one of those robes to keep from freezing.

Down three steps to the right was the main area, with three large floodlit stages, perhaps ten feet by twenty feet. Each had a stripper pole in the middle, and customer chairs all around. Against the back wall was a deejay booth for playing the necessary music. There was also a VIP area with its own stage and pole, where guys could pay more to have nicer furniture and their own private bathroom.

Then to the left were the alcoves, where private, one-on-one lap dances would happen, for an additional charge.

Dary, our colleague, and I were silent, trying to take everything in as Aaron gave the tour. Soon he led us back behind the deejay booth through a doorway and down a hall. Along one side were the well-stocked and locked storage cabinets filled with whiskey, gin, and other alcoholic beverages.

When we passed through a second doorway, we entered the locker room. Again, it was a dirty, nasty place with only a concrete floor. In the middle was an oversized vanity setup—a mirror some six feet long with bulb lights all around—where the dancers did their makeup before going onstage. Surrounding on all sides were rows and rows of metal lockers.

I was stunned as I stared at several with pictures of children taped onto the metal doors. Who were the boys and girls in these photographs? In another moment it hit me: these were the kids these women were trying to feed and clothe by working in this place.

A knot began to tighten in my throat. Here, behind the scenery of what men viewed as a sensuous house of glamour, was the total opposite. A lot of these women came here night after night trying to hold their lives together.

The room reeked of a certain overused perfume. (To this day, if I pick up that scent from any woman wearing that brand, it puts a tear in my eye.) I learned later that in the winter, the room wasn't adequately heated, so the dancers would shiver until they could get out onto the stages. In the summer the air-conditioning (actually, just a "swamp cooler") didn't work.

Nearby was another smaller locker room for the girls with the most seniority, where they had their own private bathroom. And finally, there was the manager's office.

> A knot began to tighten in my throat. Here, behind the scenery of what men viewed as a sensuous house of glamour, was the total opposite.

A Crazy Notion

We were speechless as we followed Aaron back through the main room and toward the entrance. Again, I stared at the stages, the poles, the lounge chairs. I shuddered at the thought of men my age sitting around drinking and ogling *somebody's daughter, sister, granddaughter, wife, mom*dIt just wrecked me on the inside.

"Well, Aaron, we will think and pray about this," Dary finally said, shaking his hand. At least I think that's what he said; my brain was churning. We then turned toward our car and got inside. As

Dary started the engine, he looked at me and noticed tears in my eyes. I looked at him and uttered one sentence, my voice cracking as I spoke:

"Dary . . . we have to do this, and I want to put my name in the hat to lead it."

I hadn't thought through the ramifications. I hadn't calculated how much money this would require. I hadn't weighed what it would mean, here at age forty-nine, for my very comfortable (and desirable) career at Timberline, where I enjoyed a great deal of respect as well as flexibility. Good grief, I hadn't even yet talked to my wife about this.

Plus, I'd never planted a church before. My entire ministerial career had been in established congregations. But I knew this had to happen.

Dary stared at me for a moment, his face a puzzlement. The first word out of his mouth was "Really?"

"Yeah," I replied. Thereafter, the car was mostly quiet as we drove back to our well-furnished, handsomely carpeted offices. I walked up to my second-floor office, looked out the expansive windows across the Fort Collins horizon, and then picked up my phone to call my wife. She was two hours south in Colorado Springs, taking care of her father, whose late-stage cancer was worsening by the week.

"Honey, I need to tell you what's been happening here," I began. I described the building, the possibility of starting something entirely new there, and how moved I had been by it all.

She and I had received previous inquiries from other congregations in the past few years to come be their senior pastor, but we had never felt led to follow up. This, however, was very different. In a way it tied in to our early years in youth ministry when I'd led a weekly Bible study at the local juvenile detention center. A number of kids had gotten saved. Once discharged, these gang members and their friends had started showing up in our youth group meetings at the church, to the point that we had to have a police officer on hand just for safety's sake. (Some of the clean-cut church kids and their mothers were a bit unnerved by all this.)

Now Joy, who had loved this ministry to kids on the edge, replied, "Well, to be honest, what you're talking about sounds terrifying. But God might be in this." We said we would talk more about the possibility as soon as she came back to Fort Collins.

Meanwhile, Dary and I kept talking about my crazy notion. We wrote down Aaron's asking prices: $720,000 (driven by an earlier appraisal) for this dilapidated 7,300-square-foot building in the Mulberry Corridor, plus another mandatory $300,000 for the business itself to compensate them for lost revenue.

In a couple of weeks Dary reached out to some key donors at Timberline. We described what we had seen on the tour and talked about how God might redeem this dark place in our city, turning it into a beacon of light. Their hearts were moved as they began to see the vision of what could be. Their generosity could make it possible to purchase the building and buy out the business.

While we were grateful for this breakthrough, Joy and I knew we still had a long way to go. The renovation costs would be high, and we would need to raise money for start-up and operating costs. But we knew God was calling us to reach broken, hurting people, including those who

> God was calling us to reach broken, hurting people, including those who patronized the Hunt Club as well as those who worked there.

patronized the Hunt Club as well as those who worked there. We wouldn't scare them off with the word *church*. Instead, we would call it the Genesis Project—"a place of new beginnings."

Over the spring and summer hundreds of people from Timberline Church gave sacrificially through a giving campaign toward this new endeavor, thanks to the leadership of Dary Northrop. It was clear God was up to something.

Closing the Deal

My last day at Timberline was September 30, a few weeks after the papers had been signed. The actual closing of the club had been awkward, to say the least. Aaron's brother, who was running the club while Aaron did the bookkeeping, called everyone together at 2:00 a.m. on a Saturday night (actually, early on a Sunday morning), as they were changing clothes and getting ready to leave.

"Hey, everybody, I have something to tell you," he announced. "It's all over. My brothers and I have sold this building, and we're closing—as of right now. You can come back tomorrow afternoon and clean out your lockers."

Whaaat? Dancers, bartenders, and waitstaff were shocked. They had gotten no warning that their income was lurching to a halt. Some of them had been pulling down good money—a lot of it in cash (through tips) and therefore untaxed. Now what would they do?

My heart was broken. We wanted this church to help people, not hurt them. But to them, I was the cause of putting them out on the street. No doubt they hated me and everything I stood for at that moment. They couldn't just go and get hired at another strip club across town; there weren't any. What could they do?

Some of them headed off to clubs in Denver, or Cheyenne, Wyoming, about forty-five minutes north. But others couldn't see their way clear to leave town. My friend Mark Orphan, missions pastor at Timberline (who now serves as executive pastor at the Genesis Project in Fort Collins), found a donor who was willing to give a large sum of money to help former employees with the transition. When our offer was extended, some twenty of them took us up on it, allowing us to help with everything from rent and utilities to groceries, counseling, and even tuition for going back to school.

Aaron told me at one point—with tears—that in earlier years, while his father was still alive, his job had been to recruit good-looking coeds from CSU. "I had the spiel down better than any door-to-door salesman," he said regretfully. "I told them that they could graduate debt-free by working just a few nights a week. Some of them would, but I knew most would end up dropping out of school, sucked into the vacuum of the business, destroying their futures."

Though the club had very strict policies against drugs and prostitution, there were still drug sales that happened. A former dealer who sold drugs at the club attends our church now, and former dancers have told me that sometimes dancers would go home with clients.

The three brothers each received $100,000 from the proceeds of the business. Aaron promptly turned around and donated his slice back to Timberline—even though he and his wife were hardly making ends meet themselves. He had enrolled in a master's degree program at Colorado Christian University to study counseling, while his wife was also in school. They had needed to sell their home and downsize into a place that had no Wi-Fi; they shared a laptop between them. But they were committed to pursuing a new life in Jesus, regardless of the cost.

Turning On the Light

The building became for us a metaphor of what God might do in people's broken lives. He would take all that was dirty, ugly, and shameful, redeeming it for a great kingdom purpose. The remodeling took all of 2014 and cost around $650,000, as we pretty much had to gut the building and start over, with all-new electrical, heating, and air-conditioning systems. It would have cost even more than that amount had it not been for wonderful contractors and subcontractors who donated material, or labor, or both. A drywall company owned by a Christian believer did the whole drywall job—then wrote us a check for 100 percent of his profit. I was amazed.

Here in this run-down, beat-up, shadowy place where so many dreams had died, God was getting ready to turn on the light of the good news. I had men coming to me with tears in their eyes saying things like "I'm so thankful for what this place is becoming . . . because I lost my marriage here."

One young man, a student at CSU, had been married just two years when a friend had invited him to a bachelor party at the Hunt Club. That very first night, he was smitten with one of the dancers. He eventually left his wife to marry the girl. Both of them soon got addicted to methamphetamines. He started selling, got arrested, and wound up in prison for a term. Once he was released, he and the dancer had a child together, but soon thereafter divorced.

Eventually he came to faith in Jesus. He made a point to come and tell me, "This place stole ten years of my life. Now I'm so very grateful it's been redeemed for something good."

> The building became for us a metaphor of what God might do in people's broken lives.

No Pit Too Deep

While all the remodeling was going on, I was busy assembling what I called a "launch team" of people who could help once we moved in. We met for a full year in a coffee shop in Old Town, the trendy strip of boutiques, cafés, antique shops, and confectionaries along both sides of College Avenue just north of the CSU campus.

During that year, I worked hard at persuading well-intentioned "church people" *not* to come along with us. I didn't want the Genesis Project to be viewed simply as "Timberline North" even though Timberline was being very generous to help us with operating costs. This ministry, however, would not be a good fit for people looking for just another branch of a megachurch, with everything functioning well and in order. Our work was going to be unavoidably "messy."

In fact, I kept hammering the point that *all* of us were in some ways messy and broken. This new venture could *not* be a place where nice, respectable, well-organized Christians did their bit for the "less fortunate." There would be no *us* versus *them* at the Genesis Project. We all needed to admit that we stood in equal need of God's grace.

So people came and went during that year. The ones who stayed—some eighty or ninety individuals—truly bought into our values. They believed with all their hearts that God could redeem messed-up lives. They embraced the theology of the famous quote attributed to Betsie ten Boom, who died in a Nazi concentration camp in late 1944, but not before speaking this line to her sister Corrie: "There is no pit so deep that He is not deeper still."[1]

As our intent became more widely known (the local newspaper even did a feature on it), people in need began to drop by the coffee shop gatherings. I found myself struggling at times to express to them the hope that could be found in Jesus while simultaneously prepping my launch team of established Christians. Regardless, a number of visitors came to Jesus during that year. I even baptized some of them in a horse trough!

One young woman was invited by a friend. She had endured a horribly abusive childhood; in fact, her mother was certifiably insane. Nobody in her family went to church; her parents hated church.

She never forgot the day when she was thirteen years old, huddling in her darkened room to muffle the yelling and fighting in the rest of the house. In that moment she heard an audible voice: *Life is going to be hard for you. But when you turn twenty-seven, a man will come into your life, and he will change everything.*

She assumed that if she could just hang on for fourteen more years, she would get married, and all would be better.

Daily life continued to spiral out of control for her. She was terribly insecure. One bright moment popped up in her senior year of high school, when a popular guy asked her to go to the prom. She was surprised and elated. She came up with a fancy dress. But by the end of the night, he had date-raped her. He never spoke to her again.

Years later a friend invited her to our coffee shop gathering. On her second Sunday I preached something about the love of God. (I honestly don't remember the sermon, but she can tell you the exact Scripture verse.) She remembers, "All of a sudden, it made sense to me. I prayed that day to give my life to Jesus."

She was twenty-seven years old.

"I had no idea," she told me later, "that the 'man' who would come into my life would be Jesus!"

Today she works as a county probation officer and is married to a wonderful man.

This kind of transformation has kept happening ever since.

We moved into the building and started services (double services) on February 8, 2015. My good friend and coauthor of this book, Matt Roberts, came over from Utah to speak that day. A year later the two services became three.

Meanwhile, ministry throughout the week has blossomed in and around our building. For example, we do a thing called "Kids' Café" so that low-income children from the adjacent trailer park and elsewhere who qualify for reduced- or no-cost lunches during the school year can come our way throughout the summer for a midday meal. They freely laugh and play in that same parking lot where crimes once went down.

During the school year, these same kids are dropped off at our building after classes to get homework help (and a snack) until Mom or Dad returns from work. It's a partnership we've set up with another nonprofit in the city called the Matthews House. I have to tell you, I honestly love this ministry, even when I'm driving back to our building in the midafternoon and get stuck behind that school bus!

When I talk about the work these days, I sometimes get frustrated when I choke up. But I've never been happier in my life, and neither has Joy. I told her long ago, "I simply have to be a part of something that makes me cry when I talk about it."

There's a scripture that absolutely nails it for me, where the apostle Paul wrote, "I am *obligated* [the old King James Version puts it even more bluntly, "I am *debtor*"] both to Greeks and non-Greeks, both to the wise and the foolish."[2] Yes, some people do foolish things with their lives. They make foolish choices. They should have known better. But I believe I'm *obligated* to them. I *owe* them something. Like Paul went on to explain, I owe them "the gospel, because it is the power of God that brings salvation to everyone who believes."[3]

Whether people shoot themselves in the foot repeatedly or only seldom, they all—we all—can find hope and new life in Jesus. He is, indeed, the doorway to new beginnings.

2

IMMERSED IN A
MESSY WORLD

Can any of us imagine what it must have been like for the pure, holy, righteous, immaculate Son of God to leave heaven and come down to a disgusting, messed-up, unfair, diseased, broken world?

And not just for a weekend speaking tour. Jesus came here to *live* and, eventually, to die. One popular paraphrase of John 1:14 puts it this way: "The Word became flesh and blood, and moved into the neighborhood."[1]

Couldn't he at least have hovered overhead at a safe distance? Surely the God of the universe could have chosen a more sterile route to save his fallen, rebellious, broken creation.

No. He settled in. He grew up, day upon day, year after year, in a dusty corner of the oppressive Roman Empire. He saw from an early age all that was wrong, so wrong, about society. He watched people ruining both their own lives and the lives of others. He heard the cries of pain, despair, and anger.

Then came the day when, as a young adult, he chose to go public in his hometown synagogue. He stood up and declared his manifesto, his reason for even being on this planet, by reading from the prophet Isaiah:

> The Spirit of the Sovereign LORD is on me,
>> because the LORD has anointed me
>> to proclaim good news to the poor.
>
> He has sent me to bind up the brokenhearted,
>> to proclaim freedom for the captives
>> and release from darkness for the prisoners,
>
> to proclaim the year of the LORD's favor.[2]

So *that's* what the incarnation was about: declaring good news to the poor, binding up the brokenhearted, proclaiming freedom to captives (fill in here whatever entrapment or addiction you want), and releasing prisoners out of darkness.

He did it time and again. When people criticized him for having dinner at the house of a tax collector, he said, "It is not the healthy who need a doctor, but the sick. I have not come to call the righteous, but sinners to repentance."[3] When he showed up in Jericho to the applause of adoring crowds, he didn't seem to be waving and smiling; instead, he was scanning the tree branches for the short little rip-off artist whom everyone despised. On the spot, he invited himself to Zacchaeus's house for a meal, explaining at the end, "For the Son of Man came to seek and to save the lost."[4]

He told a story about a fancy banquet to which a number of nice, respectable people were invited. Several of them, however, just couldn't manage to clear their busy calendars and show up. The frustrated host got so ticked off that he ordered, "Go out quickly into the streets and alleys of the town and bring in the poor, the crippled, the blind and the lame. . . . so that my house will be full."[5]

Out of the Christian Cul-de-Sac

Let's get honest and admit that many of us who were raised in churches—well-organized, nicely equipped, growing churches—don't do *messy* very well. We've been conditioned to want a safe environment that keeps evil out—what Gary Haugen, the Harvard-trained attorney who now leads International Justice Mission, calls "the Christian cul-de-sac." This is where "we tend to imagine most people live like us. We know life has struggles, but we figure most go about their days like we do, keeping our kids healthy and safe, advancing in our jobs, tidying up our yards, enjoying the holidays, hanging out with friends."[6]

Cul-de-sacs were designed by suburban planners to create safety for kids. If there were no through traffic, they reasoned, children would be better served. But after decades of experience, the statistics show that more children are hit by cars backing out of driveways than by cars going forward on the street.[7] Some cities are now prohibiting cul-de-sacs in their new developments because they've been proven, in fact, to be dangerous.

Is this a metaphor for many of our Christian congregations? Are we perhaps at risk of spiritual atrophy because we've shielded ourselves from people not like us?

Tim Keller, award-winning author

Let's get honest and admit that many of us who were raised in churches—well-organized, nicely equipped, growing churches—don't do *messy* very well.

and New York City pastor, has given a YouTube talk in which he says succinctly that many of us are not, as Jesus said in his opening sentence of the Sermon on the Mount, "poor in spirit."[8] We're more "middle-class in spirit."[9] That's just the way we perceive and define ourselves. We believe we bring something to the table, as though Jesus didn't have to work as hard to rescue us as he does for some of those *other* people. We naturally like feeling successful and being around other successful people.

But when we recognize our own spiritual bankruptcy, it changes how we view other people. *None* of us can pull ourselves up by our own bootstraps. It took the same sacrifice at Calvary to rescue you and me as it took to rescue the lowest drug addict.

Many of us face a constant temptation to make the American dream synonymous with the mission of God's kingdom. It's hard to lay aside our cultural baggage and take Jesus (the renegade) at face value. Be honest: Would you want to associate with the group of believers in Corinth, of whom Paul said, "Not many of you were wise by human standards; not many were influential; not many were of noble birth. . . . God chose the lowly things of this world and the despised things—and the things that are not—to nullify the things that are, so that no one may boast before him."[10]

Moving into messy places is not natural. It's against everything we've been taught to do. It certainly wasn't what I (Matt) and my lovely bride had in mind coming up through ministerial training in the late 1990s. We had both grown up in stable Christian families that took us to solid churches every week. Now we were being educated in how to make a church grow. It seemed like all of us ambitious Bible college students were laser-focused on getting our diplomas and landing positions at the biggest churches that would have us, so we could work our way up to be lead pastors of the largest churches possible. I honestly remember one guidance counselor telling me, "You don't want to start out at a small, struggling church because that's just going to stifle the trajectory of your career in the ministry."

Sure enough, as graduation neared, Candice and I were flown out to my home church in Colorado to interview for the youth pastor position. So far, so good. The offer was extended, and we readily said yes. This would be the first stepping-stone toward our future.

None of us can pull ourselves up by our own bootstraps. It took the same sacrifice at Calvary to rescue you and me as it took to rescue the lowest drug addict.

We had already made a U-Haul reservation when the phone rang. "I'm so sorry," said the senior pastor, "but something has changed here. I've decided to resign my position at this church, and so I need to rescind the offer for you to join our staff. That's a decision that should be left to the next senior pastor."

Oh. Now what? We hadn't sent out any other résumés. All our eggs were in this one basket.

In the course of time my uncle, the pastor of an inner-city church in Portland, Oregon, reached out to us (took pity on us!) and invited us to come do youth ministry there. "This is a 'building' situation," he explained diplomatically, "and we're just trying to make a difference in this community." The congregation wasn't exactly flourishing, I knew, and Portland was the cultural opposite of the Bible Belt, for sure. But with excitement and a little bit of fear, we accepted.

We rolled into town and rented a row house just off busy Southeast Eighty-Second Avenue, a very mixed neighborhood. One day Candice walked down to the nearby grocery store to pick up some things. On her way back a homeless man began following her and talking to her. The faster she walked, the more aggressive his remarks became. He followed her right up the front steps and into our living room! Fortunately I was home that day. He was high on some drug, but I didn't know that at the time.

Our evening form of entertainment became looking out the front window as the police's paddy wagon rolled up and parked each night, sending out a young female officer dressed seductively to elicit customers. Within minutes the other cops would start snagging johns and filling up the vehicle. When they had arrested six or seven—a van full—they'd drive off to the nearby precinct station to book them on solicitation charges. The next night they'd be back again.

This neighborhood obviously had its brokenness.

A Tentative Start

For my church responsibilities, I had arrived with a series of youth messages all set to deliver at the Wednesday night meetings. The only trouble was, there weren't any teenagers! We'd get set up for a seven o'clock start, and it would be just the two of us, plus maybe a couple of young twentysomethings who came to "encourage us." Across the street from the church was a group home for the developmentally disabled, and some of them would come. Not exactly the crowd that would draw high school students to attend.

Desperate to make contacts, I decided to volunteer at the high school three blocks away. This school was not exactly the cream of the city's roster, so they were glad to have somebody willing to coach freshman wrestling for free. Candice and I started to meet kids, show them love, and bring them lots of pizza.

What we quickly came to realize was that these weren't "bad" kids; they were simply reflections of the broken families and the broken world in which they lived. I was both amazed and appalled to learn that some of these kids—as young as fourteen—were basically living at home alone. They had no reason to be interested in church. But they responded to us as people. We didn't have to be cool. We just showed them we cared. And when we told them about our Wednesday night thing, they said, "Sure, why not?"

Whenever I spoke, I kept repeating the point that "Jesus *loves* you! When nobody else out there cares about you, guess what: You *do* have a Father in heaven. He's always on your side, watching over you and taking care of you."

Some of them would wander into the church as early as 3:45 in the afternoon, as soon as school was out. They'd do homework or just hang out until the evening meeting—after which I'd need to give them a ride home in the church's sixteen-passenger van. Their parents were obviously not going to come pick them up.

One night still sticks in my memory. It was late—past ten o'clock—when we got to Tara's place. Tara was around fifteen years old. As soon as we rounded the corner, we saw police lights flashing. They had set up a barricade around her house because her stepdad was holding a gun to her mom's head, threatening to kill her and then himself.

An officer came out to talk to Tara.

> They had no reason to be interested in church. But they responded to us as people. We didn't have to be cool. We just showed them we cared.

He assured her that her two younger sisters had been extracted from the house and were safe in a squad car. Now they were trying to get the stepdad to drop the weapon.

My first instinct was, *Oh, this is so terrible! I've got to console this poor girl.*

She looked blankly at me with an attitude of, *Eh . . . it happens all the time. Here we go again. He won't actually kill her. He never does.*

The police officer said to Tara, "Can you take your little sisters with you?"

"Yeah," she replied in a deadpan tone. "I'll take them."

As the officer turned away, I couldn't help asking, "Where are you going to go?"

"I don't know," she murmured. "I'll figure something out."

"Why don't you guys come with me?" I said. "We'll help you." And so we ended up with three young girls on couches in the church's youth room that night.

Today, I'm glad to report, Tara is an incredible young woman who loves Jesus. In fact, she's married to my cousin.

"You Gotta Hear This!"

Candice and I had become immersed in this world of chaos and need. Four of my young wrestlers started coming to Wednesday night meetings. Pretty much the first time I gave an altar call, all four of them promptly got up and came forward, almost like a pack. Soon they were crying and praying at the front.

From that point onward, they would grab their friends at school and say, "Hey, you're coming to church with us. You gotta come hear this!" They didn't even give the kid a choice in the matter. Before we knew it, the auditorium was filling up . . . a hundred kids, then two hundred, then three hundred. It was crazy.

One time they brought the roughest, toughest guy in school, the captain of the football team. And when I got to the climax of my message and called for response, the four wrestlers said to him, "All right—come on. You're going up there!" The next thing I knew, this big hulk of a kid was bawling his eyes out, giving himself to Jesus, while his nose was leaking like a sieve.

It got to the point that kids would say to me, "Hey, I want to preach next week." Really? Sure enough, they would get up and try to explain the gospel to their peers. It wasn't polished, but kids would respond just the same.

In 2001, we chose to do a See You at the Pole event in early September, when kids would gather for prayer around the school flagpole before classes started. Four hundred kids showed up.

The very next week brought the shock of September 11. On the West Coast (three hours behind New York and Washington), we awoke to the awful news reports. At first, I thought it might be an elaborate hoax, but I learned it was all too real as the morning crawled on. We were sitting together as a small church staff, huddled around a TV, taking in every bit of news, when my phone rang. It was the assistant principal at the high school.

"Pastor Matt," he said in a troubled voice, "will you come over and speak to our students?"

I took a deep breath, trying to think of how to respond. In the back of my mind, I knew how secular the Portland public schools were, how wary of anything religious. Finally I said, "Actually—I don't know how to do that. Given the restrictions, I have nothing to say. I can't."

He wouldn't accept that. "You come," he insisted. "I need you here."

So I headed for the school, where I found the entire student body gathered on the bleachers in the gym. Kids were staring into space, of course, wondering what had just happened to their world. The room was much quieter than normal.

The assistant principal went to the microphone. "Okay, everyone," he said, "listen up. All teachers will be dismissed now to go to [room such-and-such]; we're going to have a staff meeting. While we're away, I have asked Matt Roberts to be here today and share a few words with our students."

I honestly cannot remember what I said that day. Something about hope—where does it come from on a day like this? I think I eventually got around to saying, "This is your opportunity to find ways to make a difference in our messed-up world. In fact, God created you for a larger purpose." And then I prayed that God would calm our fears and help our ravaged country.

There was never a time when my wife and I looked at each other and said we had changed—but we had. The needs of that community became ours. We stayed there for four and a half years, during which time our first two sons were born. We were entirely swept up in connecting with needy teenagers and their messed-up families.

When church members would occasionally complain to me about stains on the sanctuary carpet or cigarette butts in the parking lot, I would just smile and say, "Yes—I know! Isn't it awesome?"

Finding Our Place

The point when Candice and I *did* notice our change of perspective was when we moved from Portland to Denver for seminary and I took an associate pastor position at a suburban church. It wasn't a bad church by any measure. But one of my jobs was to call on first-time visitors. They would quiz me with things like, "Well, what do you have for _____?" and "What kind of programs are you running for _____?" They were basically church shopping, and I felt like a salesman trying to coax them back to our door.

I would literally go home and cry to my wife, "We messed up! I hate doing this!" Those two years are still mostly a blur in my memory. Both of us could hardly wait to get back in touch with needy people.

In 2006, through an unusual series of events, we landed in Ogden, Utah, a city of some eighty thousand people on Interstate 15, up north from Salt Lake City. This became the seedbed for planting a new kind of ministry—"a church for people who don't do church," we said. We're still there today. Some people have wondered if clean-cut, decent Utah, with its well-ordered Mormon majority, even has broken people in need. Ogden is the early home of such notables as J. Willard Marriott, of hotel fame, and also Donny and Marie Osmond. But the truth is, *every* community across the nation, no matter how prestigious, has a soft underbelly of dysfunction and pain—as the stories throughout the rest of this book will illustrate.

We didn't bother digging out old how-to-plant-a-church books and lecture notes. We just started loving the people whom nobody else wanted to love. And we found that when we immersed ourselves in the world of those who were desperate and hurting, they spread the word. We didn't have to advertise. We didn't have to buy billboards or TV commercials. We didn't have to think up clever ways to invite people to church. We just represented the face of Jesus to those who were a hot mess.

In so doing, we joined with what Jesus said about his mission that day in the Nazareth synagogue. If he had kept reading further in Isaiah 61, he would have come to these words:

> To comfort all who mourn,
>   and provide for those who grieve in Zion—
> to bestow on them a crown of beauty
>   instead of ashes,
> the oil of joy
>   instead of mourning,
> and a garment of praise
>   instead of a spirit of despair.
> They will be called oaks of righteousness,
>   a planting of the LORD
>   for the display of his splendor.
>
> They will rebuild the ancient ruins
>   and restore the places long devastated;
> they will renew the ruined cities
>   that have been devastated for generations.[11]

Broken people today, beneath their drugs and rap sheets and alcoholism and conflicted relationships, are in mourning. Their lives are a pile of ashes. In many cases they have been long "devastated for generations."

Jesus comes into their reality to bring "a crown of beauty . . . the oil of joy . . . a garment of praise." He is (to use a title to which we church folks have become almost numb) the *Redeemer*. He takes back what has been scuffed up and makes it shine again.

Close Enough to Touch

One of the most over-the-top scenes in the ministry of Jesus was when a leper approached him for healing. His highly contagious disease made him isolated in the ancient world; no one dared to get near him. But Scripture says, "Jesus reached out his hand and *touched* the man."[12] He didn't just speak to him from ten yards away. He made himself ceremonially unclean by actually putting his fingers on rotting, oozing flesh.

This man had not known the sensation of human touch for years. Now, in a moment, Someone came close to him with healing, cleansing power. His life was revolutionized that day.

Sometimes a curious child will ask you or me, "Where is Jesus right now?" The answer, of course, is that he's everywhere (the theological term is *omnipresent*). Well, then, what's the implication for those of us who call ourselves Christ followers? He spelled it out clearly when he said, "Whoever serves me must follow me; and where I am, my servant also will be."[13]

Into the messiness of broken people's lives? Yes.

We do not go alone, of course. We go with divine empowerment. Paul Borthwick in his book *Great Commission, Great Compassion* makes an enlightening comment about Acts 1:8, in which Jesus said the Holy Spirit would propel the disciples to "be my witnesses in Jerusalem, and in all Judea and Samaria, and to the ends of the earth." Borthwick defines "Samaria" in the following way:

Those who are geographically near but culturally distant, including those we have been taught to fear or even hate. Who are our Samaritans? For some it's undocumented immigrants. For

29

others it could be prisoners or former prisoners. Some fear or hate people from other religions—especially those who we might assume are "radical" or extremists. And for many it's the LGBT community.[14]

In other words, people who are nearby but not exactly like us. People whom Jesus came to reach and change. People whom Jesus loves. His power is more than up to the task. We get the privilege of plunging into the world's muck along with him and making an eternal difference.

PART TWO

WHAT REDEMPTION LOOKS LIKE

IN THIS SECTION WE DELVE INTO THE ESSENTIAL components of bringing broken people toward stability before God. These are in no way intended to be a scientific formula, with an implied guarantee of success. They are instead organic in nature—a set of windows, if you will, through which redemption can come into focus.

3

WE PURSUE REAL
RELATIONSHIPS

The first time Jay Salas showed up at one of our Friday night meetings, I (Matt) could tell right away that he'd lived a hard life. He looked to be no older than thirty, but he was already missing a number of teeth, probably from methamphetamine use (I assumed). His frame was gaunt. He was tattooed from head to toe.

A friend of a friend had invited him, saying, "It's just a come-as-you-are kind of place. And it has free coffee," which never hurts. Still, Jay hung around the shadows of the room, fearful of making conversation with anyone.

I was encouraged, though, to see him come back a week or two later. Maybe he sensed something good about being with us. He kept showing up. I said to him at one point, "Hey, I'd love to just hang out sometime. Let's get together this week."

"Uh, well, I don't know . . ." he softly responded. I didn't push him.

But apparently, I hadn't scared him off, because he showed up again after that. I kept extending the low-key invitation to do lunch. It took close to three months before he said yes.

Once we sat down in the fast-food restaurant, I began the conversation by asking, "So what's going on in your life? What's your story?"

Jay stared down at his food for a while; then his eyes began darting around the place. Finally, he summoned the courage to speak.

Trust Precedes Truth

It is a universal fact of life that none of us—rich or poor, stable or in chaos—engages very freely with people we don't trust. What if they start scolding us or make us feel stupid? What if they take our words and twist them to their own advantage? What if they're wanting to get money out of us? It's only natural for us to be cautious at first.

For people who carry a load of personal junk, this is doubly true. They've repeatedly been messed with by others with ill motives. They're embarrassed by bad choices they've made in the past. They may be afraid of the police. They may have been disowned by parents or other family members.

They certainly do not feel anywhere near qualified to approach a holy God. The very thought of that is downright scary to them. When a Christian says, "Jesus wants to be in a relationship with you," that is 100 percent true—but all they can think of are the broken, booby-trapped, unhealthy relationships they have known in life up to that point. They're not sure anymore what a positive relationship would even look like.

Christians are fond of saying about their faith, "It's not about religion—it's about relationship." Well, *both* of those words can be terrifying to those who are troubled. Inside their heads, they're thinking, *I for sure don't want religion, and I don't deserve relationship.*

Thus the starting point for any kind of redemption is to find another human being who's not fake or faux or manipulative but real. If people think they're worth your care and—could it be?—your love, that would be amazing. To get to know someone who is not going to quickly look down on them or condemn them would be a dream come true.

And, over time, this can become a catalyst for lasting change. We have a saying at the Genesis Project that goes like this: "Relationship is a gospel conduit." It's the pipeline that lets the gospel flow freely.

The New Testament calls God's people in nineteen different places to love one another.[1] Love drains out our prejudices, breaks apart our pigeon-holed ways of thinking, and draws us to see one another as unique people. We get to know more about the other people, the forces that have shaped them, the aches that linger deep inside, the longings for a future that's better than the past.

> **Christians are fond of saying about their faith, "It's not about religion—it's about relationship." Well, *both* of those words can be terrifying to those who are troubled.**

The Whole Load

Somehow Jay Salas had arrived at the point of thinking he could trust me. So he decided at that lunch table to tell me his story—the whole load of the good, the bad, and the ugly.

"I grew up here in Ogden," he began, "and joined a gang by the time I was fourteen. One night we were cruising down Washington Boulevard [the city's main north-south strip] when a kid from a rival gang stuck his head out the car window and began to shout expletives our way. I pulled my nine-millimeter handgun out of my pocket, closed my eyes, and fired into the other car until the gun was empty.

"That night my life would change forever. I was arrested and then charged with attempted murder (luckily, the kid I had shot survived his wounds). I found myself being bounced around between juvenile and adult prisons as I awaited trial. I felt lost, confused, and all alone. When my trial finally came, it had been decided that, at fourteen years old, I would be charged as a juvenile, not as an adult. I was found guilty and turned over to state custody."

As this man kept talking, it almost seemed as if he was testing me, to see if I really wanted to know him or not. If he shocked me strongly enough, maybe he could scare me off.

He went on to describe how, upon his release from the juvenile system, the authorities had said, in essence, that he wasn't allowed to stay around Ogden anymore. Instead, the State placed him in a proctor home at the other end of Utah, more than six hours away from the only place he had ever known as home.

With no family or support system, he continued down the very dangerous road of violence and addiction. After a while, he met a young woman named Sherey, who had a very young daughter at the time. They soon got married, had a baby together, and then another one, all the while living on welfare and struggling to get by. Any amount of money Jay earned seemed to be quickly spent on an all-consuming drug addiction he couldn't seem to kick, no matter how hard he tried.

So many things continued to haunt Jay . . . like when Sherey had called to say she was at the hospital about to deliver their son, Jay Jr., he was so high on meth he imagined her words to be a concocted lie from the police to entrap him. After all, he'd already been in and out of jail on various charges of drug possession as well as dealing. Now he ran, afraid—missing the birth of his only son. When Jay finally did show up at the hospital, he was so belligerent and out of control that the police had to be called. He was arrested and spent the next six months in county jail.

Jay had dealt with uncontrollable anger throughout his life. This anger often caused him to act out in physical and emotional abuse toward his family. He was carrying the guilt of chronically abusing and cheating on his wife throughout their marriage, in both heterosexual and homosexual affairs. And at the root of all this mess was a drug addiction that had poisoned every corner of his life.

Now the family of five had found their way back to Ogden. Unfortunately a change of scenery didn't change much for Jay and Sherey. He had landed in jail for drugs and domestic violence more than once since their return. The cycle of destruction and hopelessness just kept repeating itself.

An Impossible Dream?

As Jay kept dumping his story on me at lunch, I sensed it was almost as if he wanted to imply, *This is who I am. This is my identity. It's what I do.*

When he finally got to a pause, I said, "So tell me why you're here. What are you looking for, Jay?"

He bit his lip for a moment, then answered, "I guess what I want is peace. And the only way I can imagine to get it is to kill myself. But I'm too big of a coward to do it." And he began to cry.

I spoke about hope and forgiveness through Jesus. "If you were allowed to hope for something," I asked, "what would it be?"

"A life without all this pain," he said. "But that kind of hope seems impossible."

"What if I told you that I hope the same thing for you too? But I do believe it's possible."

At this, he cried all the harder.

I didn't press the spiritual point any further that day; we'd plowed through a lot. But soon after that, I was heading to Colorado for some meetings, and I invited him to ride along. This would give us seven or more hours together each way in the car.

He said yes. So I told him where and when to meet me on the given day.

But he stood me up. I was disappointed, of course.

He told me later, "I'm so sorry—but I was just afraid. When I had first come to the Genesis Project, what seemed so real about you and everybody else just scared the hell out of me. It terrified me. People like you had never wanted to be around me before. I didn't understand why you guys were different from all the rest."

I didn't react to the matter of the Colorado trip; I just continued befriending him, creating a space where he could feel comfortable and welcome. We did more lunches. Then one Friday night after about three or four months, I finished my sermon with a simple invitation: "If any of you want to make Jesus the centerpiece of your life, if you want to begin this journey of hope and restoration, come forward, and let's pray together."

Jay stepped out that night. Later I learned he had said a "prayer of salvation" sometime before, but was still looking for something deeper, something more. Within minutes he was weeping loudly. Our little group of sixty or seventy people surrounded him with love and prayer.

Ripple Effect

The very next week, he was back—and Sherey with him. She was very hesitant. She was not as forthcoming as her husband had been. It took some time for my wife and me to learn her story: how she had been orphaned on the Navajo reservation, how a pastor and his family had taken her into their home and raised her there, but how the turmoil of her earlier years and the abandonment she felt had never left her. When I would preach on a certain parable of Jesus, she would come and sit with me afterward to say, "You know, here is how my grandpa [actually the pastor who had raised her] used to tell me that story." She would go on repeating pieces of the sermons she had heard him preach when she was a young girl. This opened the door to our spiritual conversations under the guise of talking about her grandpa, who had passed away by then.

In the early going Sherey's opinion seemed to be, "I know enough about Jesus to know that we don't deserve this kind of love and forgiveness. We're not *these people*." But in time she softened. She and Jay even began bringing their children to our services. We could tell the kids were wary about the change in their dad—the man who had neglected them and abused their mother, who had burned through their family's money by doing drugs right in front of them, but who now talked enthusiastically about Jesus. As he would wholeheartedly engage in worship, they seemed to be eyeing him, as if waiting for the other shoe to drop.

But the change in Jay Salas's life was real. It was permanent. The rest of his family eventually joined him in following Jesus. As the years went by, his faith and his understanding of the Bible grew to the point that he founded recovery groups for those coming out of drug addiction. Today he is the full-time recovery pastor of the Genesis Project–Ogden, a dynamic minister to people as hopeless as he himself once was.

But none of this would ever have happened without a relationship that he perceived as *real*.

Can't Fake It

People who have been taken advantage of or misled in the past have especially sensitive antennae for phoniness and pretension. They are used to reading subtle signals that indicate hidden agendas.

It won't do for any of us to try to keep a brave face, masking feelings of inner revulsion. If we honestly don't like a person, we will never be slick enough to convince them otherwise. None of us are that good at "acting."

> **People who have been taken advantage of or misled in the past have especially sensitive antennae for phoniness and pretension.**

To fake acceptance or pleasantness is a dead-end street. Most people will sniff us out before long.

Instead, we have to see each person we encounter the way Jesus did—the way he reacted to the woman caught in adultery, for example. He never showed a flicker of disdain (while still recognizing the fact of her wrongdoing—see John

8:11). Instead, he deflected her would-be prosecutors. She left that encounter relieved and uplifted.

This kind of work calls us to a deep-down change, the kind the Lord offered through the prophet Ezekiel: "I will give you a new heart and put a new spirit in you; I will remove from you your heart of stone and give you a heart of flesh. And I will put my Spirit in you."[2] This is the key.

We cannot manufacture love for the chronically homeless or addicted. We have to get the heart of Jesus to love them. As the apostle John wrote, "We love because he first loved us."[3]

And isn't this how we know we are growing as disciples anyway? We're increasing in our love for God and for people—all kinds. The closer we get to him, the more we love the way he does.

Unless our hearts are truly broken, we will never bring hope to hopeless people.

What Real Relationships Are NOT

Before going further, we need to stop and take note of what we're *not* talking about when we say "real relationships" with broken people. Here are several that come to mind.

Connections Based on Affinity

A lot of church fellowship is based on getting into groups with people of like mind and like station in life. Some churches have groups for everything from parents of preschoolers to fly fishermen. They evoke the law of natural attraction. There's nothing wrong with that. But it's not going to get very far in crossing the gap into the broken and dark places of our communities.

We don't have to have a shared history with people to be in relationship with them. A funny example: One night the phone rang in the Roberts house, and a gruff voice said, "Hey, Pastor Matt! I'm having an argument with my wife. In fact, we've made a bet. She says you've never done time [in jail] and I say you have. Who's right?"

I recognized the voice as a guy who had been in and out of prison more than once. "No, actually," I replied, "I've never been locked up."

"Whaaat? Are you sure?" He didn't want to believe me.

"Yep, I'm sure," I answered.

"No way!"

I could hear his wife cackling in the background. "Ha-ha! You owe me twenty bucks!"

We don't have to have a past of doing heroin to love a drug user. We don't have to have experienced homelessness to love a homeless man or woman. We don't have to be a former alcoholic to love an alcoholic. We don't have to have abused kids ourselves to love a child abuser.

> We don't have to have a past of doing heroin to love a drug user. We don't have to have experienced homelessness to love a homeless man or woman.

Instead, we just have to be accessible and say we're willing to walk with such a person in their pain and dysfunction. That means spending time together. Love and time are inseparable. You can't tell your spouse "I love you" while not giving your time. In the same way, you can't tell a broken person you love them without being at their side.

Conditional Requirements

"I'll care about you and stick with you *if* you begin to straighten up. As long as you meet my expectations, you're going to have all of me that you want. But if you start messing up, you're going to notice me pulling back from you a little."

A lot of Christians came up through a church culture that conveyed the notion of relationships being earned. Yes, you might be struggling, and so, of course, the church would try to steer you back in the right direction. And if you didn't cooperate, the relationship would fade.

Christian bodies still practice excommunication all the time—maybe not formally but in reality. They feel they must uphold moral standards, and if you fall short, they have to remove you from fellowship. How so? By pulling back on proximity and warmth. They send the unspoken message that you're not really welcome anymore.

A version of this in the field of alcohol or drug addiction is known popularly as The Intervention. This is a specific time when the person is brought into a room where all, or at least many, of his or her closest connections are waiting: spouse, mother, father, sister, brother, work colleague, best friend. They proceed to deliver a stern message: "Your addiction is out of control. It's destroying you. You really must go into rehab—tonight! And if you don't, we're going to pull back all support from you. We're done stringing along with you."

It sounds good. But current research is starting to raise serious questions about this confrontational approach. It is showing that the best chance a troubled person has is when they're surrounded by a strong, supportive community, not only when they're sober but even when they're on a bender. The true supporter says, "Yes, your life is really hard just now. But guess what: I'm still here. I'm going to sit here and hold you while you're vomiting. I still love you.

"And the second thing I want to say is, your life is hard because of *you*! The pain is because of what you're doing to yourself. There's nobody else to blame."

So you're not coddling the person. You're not enabling the person to continue their self-destruction. You're bringing truth into the fog. But, meanwhile, you're extending unconditional love and care.

Real relationships cannot be performance based.

Structured Mentoring

You may be surprised to see this in the list of problematic arrangements. Perhaps you've had a healthy connection to an older, wiser person whom you invited into your life. You've shared your deepest questions with this individual, and you've gained valuable insights.

That is all well and good. But in our work, we get nervous whenever someone comes up and says, "Pastor, I'd like to mentor somebody. I feel like I can really help them get squared away." What's being implied here is a we-they paradigm. *They need solutions, and I have a ready supply of them. I'll be glad to impart my superior wisdom to them during an allotted time, when it's convenient for me.*

Real relationships don't work that way.

This is not to say that the two of us don't do at least some pastoral counseling during set appointments. But much more of our weeks are spent "on the fly," whenever distraught people want to talk. Their lives usually don't run on a strict schedule. Many of them wouldn't think to call the Genesis Project office and request an hour of time next Thursday morning at ten thirty. Instead, we seek to build organic relationships within the ebb and flow of people's lives.

One of the ways we do this is through our in-house coffee shops, which are open weekdays as well as Sundays. These are more than just places to grab a latte or a cappuccino; they are "discipleship venues," if you will.

"Us and them" simply doesn't work very well with broken people. It reinforces their sense of unworthiness and failure. They don't want to go to another "doctor," so to speak. They yearn instead for a genuine friend.

Service Programs/Benevolence/Handouts/Charity

This probably won't win us many accolades from churches and other nonprofit organizations. But we've noticed, after years of work in this ministry, that we rarely see long-term success for the gospel in cases that begin with giving out money. It launches the relationship on the wrong foot—another version of us and them. It says, *You're messed up, and I'll give you a little boost here.*

Christians are wired to want to write a check, to do projects for the "less fortunate." That sounds noble. But in our experience, opportunities to serve are only starting lines, not finish lines.

> "Us and them" simply doesn't work very well with broken people. It reinforces their sense of unworthiness and failure.

The apostle Peter said to the lame beggar at the temple gate, "Silver or gold I do not have, but what I do have I give you. In the name of Jesus Christ of Nazareth, walk."[4] He and his fellow apostle, John, were keyed in on what would make a genuine difference in this needy man's future.

To be clear: Yes, we rent motel rooms for homeless people on cold winter nights. We feed the hungry. We regularly rally our people together to do ROCK events (Random Outbreaks of Community Kindness), during which we put on obnoxious T-shirts and go out cleaning up yards for the elderly and fixing broken toilets. But these are not the core functions of our ministry. At week's end we don't pat ourselves on the back for having been charitable and done outreach. Instead we say we've put just a small foot in the door to try to begin connecting with people in need.

In Fort Collins we participate in a program known as FFH (Faith Family Hospitality), in which some thirty churches across the city open up their buildings to host homeless families a week at a time. Two or three times a year, we rearrange our rooms for them to have sleeping space, using cots provided by FFH; we come up with the sheets and blankets ourselves. We provide evening meals for them and breakfasts as well the next morning. We plan activities for the kids.

But we also just sit and listen to them. We eat the same food they eat, at the same tables. We work hard to treat these folks as friends.

And the outcome is that today we have probably six or more of these families who have come to Jesus and are a regular part of our church after living in our building for a week—despite the fact that our facility is probably the least accommodating. We don't have a gym. We have no showers. Our physical space is cramped. Yet time and again we've heard the comment, "This just feels like home."

Service projects are not wrong. They are simply incomplete without going further to get in touch with people's lives. And that leads us to an important truth.

Real Relationships Are Messy

You are probably figuring out by now that getting involved in the world's brokenness can become complicated. It can chew up more hours and more energy than you ever predicted. Your slick theories get jumbled. Your personal standards get violated.

We've heard Christians ask, "If I really show love and acceptance to, for instance, my brother who's a meth addict, am I condoning his behavior? He needs to know that I don't approve, doesn't he?"

Chances are he already knows that. He considers himself a scumbag in your eyes. What he lacks is any idea of how to change the picture. He thinks he could never again be okay as your sibling.

We who have lived stable, respectable lives can struggle to understand the value systems of others. Dr. Ruby K. Payne, an educator, has written about the disconnect between the poor and those who would teach them. She tells the story of a teacher who noticed a student who came to school every day with nothing but processed food in his lunch bag: candy, potato chips, soda, and the like. He wasn't doing well in his studies. She and her fellow teachers were concerned about his health. They decided to investigate and found, to their surprise, that the boy and his family lived in a trailer with no refrigerator. No wonder everything they ate was prepackaged.

The teachers got together and pooled their money to buy this family a refrigerator. When it was delivered and installed, they celebrated.

The next week the boy was absent from school all week—five days straight. When he returned the following Monday, the teacher naturally asked, "So where were you?"

Answer: "We went on vacation."

What! How in the world had this come about? With a little more probing, the teacher learned that the family had promptly sold the refrigerator for cash so they could go on a fun trip. She and her colleagues were furious, of course. How could these ungrateful parents have done something so ridiculous?

But, in fact, this family had not seen any need for a refrigerator. They had been eating okay, they'd told themselves. On the other hand, they would never, ever be able to afford a vacation. So they had made the logical choice, according to what they valued most.

In her bestselling book *A Framework for Understanding Poverty*, which has sold more than one million copies, Dr. Payne wrote, "The key to achievement for students from poverty is in creating relationships with them. . . . When students who have been in poverty (and have successfully made it into middle class) are asked how they made the journey, the answer nine times out of ten has to do with relationship—a teacher, a counselor, or coach who made a suggestion or took an interest in them as individuals."[5]

Getting involved with people in need does not always lead to happy endings. We ought to know this from the very beginning of human history. The Bible tells how God, the sovereign Creator of the world, reached out to build a relationship with the original two humans by coming down and "walking in the garden in the cool of the day."[6] He put himself close to Adam and Eve . . . and, sure enough, they messed up. God found himself rejected and wounded by their free choices. Things had not turned out at all as he had wished.

At the Genesis Project this happens to us all the time. Real relationships bleed into our lives and make a mess. The phone rings late at night, and a slurred voice says, "Rob (or Matt) . . . I'm drunk. I probably shouldn't drive home. Is there any way you could come pick me up?" Unlike in a more "respectable" church, this person isn't trying to impress their pastor or hide their failings. They're crying out for help.

I (Rob) got a phone call about a guy who had been horsing around at a party thrown by his motorcycle club, in which he was a full-patch member. ("Full patch" means you've qualified to wear the club's complete four-piece crest on your leather vest.) He had broken his leg in a fight.

I said to the friend who called me, "If he's laid up with his leg and can't work, how about if Joy and I bring him dinner?" Good idea, said the friend.

So we showed up at the guy's single-wide trailer with a warm meal. We had to push aside his bong (water pipe) on the kitchen table to make room for the food. The guy was lying there with a cast on his leg, pretty much wiped out from treating his pain with oxycodone. We stayed about fifteen minutes just talking, and then left.

To our subsequent delight, he began showing up on Sundays once his leg got better. "I knew this was a church I could go to," he told us, "because you saw all my drug paraphernalia. I was strung out, but you didn't care. You didn't judge me."

Real Relationships Are Long-Haul

Making headway in broken lives requires long-term patience. That's what makes it so hard at times. Not everybody is like Jay Salas, who turned on a dime to accept Jesus and never looked back. Many others go up and down, relapsing, and then returning to try again.

We see this all the time in our efforts in Fort Collins to love our neighbors in the trailer park immediately behind our building. It's a part of our community that is often forgotten and overlooked and not without its share of challenges. When somebody offered to donate a trailer to the church, we thought we could move it onto one of the lots and turn it into a sort of community center for helping kids with homework, running ESL classes, and so forth.

Well, it turned out that the zoning laws made this idea cost-prohibitive. We were already spending a bundle to remodel the trailer and get rid of its mold; this was becoming the most expensive "free gift" we'd ever received. To now qualify it as a place for public assembly would cost even more.

So we changed our plan. We started looking for a couple of interns to simply move in and try to build relationships among the residents. We didn't have a specific set of programs in mind. To be honest, we didn't even really know what the people needed or wanted.

We assumed the interns, if we could find them, would be guys; after all, this wasn't the safest address in town. We were surprised when two young women who were just graduating from nearby Colorado State University stepped up. They had incredible people skills, and they were willing to raise their own support for a year.

One girl had volunteered during college with a well-known youth ministry, and her supervisor was not at all impressed by this new venture. We had a pretty intense meeting. "You guys don't seem to have a plan here," her female supervisor declared. "You're going to put these girls in a dangerous situation. What kind of training are you going to provide? How are you going to keep them safe?"

We didn't have any convincing answers.

This pair of white girls from upper-middle-class backgrounds, however, soon moved in and started meeting their neighbors. Kids began hanging out at the girls' trailer. The two of them offered to help some of the kids with homework. They rounded up a bunch of the kids and took them out for a boating day on nearby Horsetooth

Reservoir. The kids had never been on open water before or had even worn a life jacket; in fact, some of them said they had never been in the mountains even though they'd lived in Colorado all their lives.

Moms began to trust these interns. They began asking questions about child-raising, despite the fact that both girls were still single and in their early twenties. Now moms were asking, "What do I do with my teenager?"

One mom, an undocumented Latina, was trying to manage three kids while working two jobs after her husband had gotten deported for some criminal act. She had to leave early in the morning and wouldn't return from washing dishes in a restaurant until two the next morning, which meant her fourteen-year-old was basically raising the younger two. Talk about a challenge.

Yet, when she heard that our ROCK week was going to send women to nursing homes to paint the nails of the residents there, this mom came knocking on our trailer door one night. Holding out a Walmart bag, she said to our intern, "I don't have much, but here's some nail polish for your event."

The girls started attending a Monday night barbecue just to encourage more relationships. (It has also proven to be a good setting for them to pick up more Spanish.) They have been fully embraced by the community. A high school teacher in our church spearheaded an effort to raise $90,000 from donors to build a nice playground and a community garden on the part of our property that borders the trailer park.

Yes, we've taken certain precautions—for example, putting a burglar alarm on the trailer. After an evening event at church, we'll walk them back home. But I've had multiple men who live in the trailer park come to me and say, "You don't have to worry about these girls. We'll take care of them if anybody tries to mess with them."

We have never had the trailer or our building spoiled with graffiti, whereas back when it was a strip club, it got tagged all the time.

I can't claim that swarms of trailer park residents have started coming to Sunday morning church, but that's never been the goal. The goal has simply been to love our literal neighbors the best we can. We're there for the long haul, building relationships. The two interns came to me after just six months and said they wanted to sign up for a second year. "We're not sure we'll ever leave here," one of them said. I'd love to hire them as full-time staff.

A Ministry for All

Building real relationships is not something for just the socially inclined or the clergy. In fact, being a pastor is, in some cases, a hindrance. Christians who don't have a title or a position are ahead in this work.

God just seems to open doors for those willing to love the people no one else wants to love. When you immerse yourself in the world of "the least of these,"[7] he entrusts you with plenty of opportunities. We (Rob and Joy) showed up for church one Sunday morning to find a drug-addicted homeless couple sitting literally on the doorstep, waiting for someone to arrive. The woman was nine months pregnant. "We didn't know what to do," they said, "but we were just heading down this street and thought maybe you could help us."

We invited them inside. By the end of the last service that day, the woman was sitting out in our coffee shop area having contractions while one of our members, a nurse, sat beside her holding her hand and timing the intervals. They drove her to the hospital, and eighty minutes later a little girl was born—drug-addicted, of course.

The authorities were not about to let this couple, in their present state, take the girl out onto the streets. Joy and I ended up providing foster care to this precious child for the next five months, after which another family in our church took our place. Only recently were the birth parents able to convince the county officials that they were stable enough to regain custody.

You don't have to have a college degree in sociology to care for people. You don't have to be ordained. You only have to be willing to love. And God takes notice of that.

God just seems to open doors for those willing to love the people no one else wants to love.

Randy and Martha Crider came to the Fort Collins Genesis Project in its early days, after being intrigued by the newspaper coverage about our buying the strip club. They called and asked to have breakfast with me. The minute I laid eyes on this sweet, soon-to-be-retired couple and heard their lovely Tennessee accent, I assumed this wouldn't work at all. Martha was a classic Southern belle. Randy was just an all-around nice, clean-cut guy. I went home and told Joy, "I had a great breakfast with these dear folks, but they'll never come to our church. If they wrote a list of what they're looking for in a church, we couldn't check one single box." To our surprise, they started showing up. They bought into the vision of building relationships with messy people.

Randy and Martha are the people who stop at the Motel 6 to pick up single moms and their kids for services. They're the ones who help look for apartments that will accept people with felonies on their record, which makes renting almost impossible. And low-income housing in our college city is in perpetual short supply.

They come to me regularly, saying, "We're in touch with so-and-so, who's got this big set of problems—what do we say? How should we help them?"

I cannot imagine our church without this couple. They genuinely love the broken and make themselves available even though nothing in their church background has been anything like our place. They've bought into the truth that if they extend simple love and friendship, God will guide them from that point onward.

Real, genuine, patient, unconditional relationships can lead to the only relationship that truly changes and heals people—a relationship with Jesus.

4

WE OPEN UP TRUE STORIES

Every living person has a story. But most would rather not expose their *stuff* to critical ears. They need to find a safe place before opening up.

Such was the case with Breck Brown, a young single mom with short, curly brown hair who began coming to the Genesis Project–Ogden during its earlier days. We enjoyed her bubbly, outgoing personality. The Sunday dedication of her baby daughter to the Lord before the whole congregation was a joyous moment.

She joined a recovery group, without saying much about what her particular issues were. I (Matt) didn't press her, and neither did the rest of our team. She could be allowed to talk whenever she was ready.

The church was growing to the point that we needed more space, and so in 2015, we relocated to a former Coca-Cola bottling plant that we could remodel. Along with the main building came several little bungalows across the street that were part of the package. Various renters were living there, and so we needed to honor the rest of their leases before doing anything further.

The larger seating capacity was a blessing, and the crowd kept growing. But somewhere along the way, I realized we weren't seeing Breck very much anymore. Where had she gone? It couldn't have been a distance problem; we were now only a couple of miles south of the previous place. I sent her text messages to follow up, and she would text back: Sorry—I've been busy. She would come to church once or twice; then we wouldn't see her for long stretches.

Reconnection

Every summer our church does a special week called Wanna Give Away (a shameless knockoff of the Southwest Airlines catchphrase *Wanna Get Away*), during which we tackle all kinds of work projects. Some are for the benefit of neighbors in need, while others are for the church itself. One of these was to clean up the one bungalow that had no lease in effect, with the aim of turning it into a recovery house for guys truly intent on making a clean start in life.

We had found out, to our dismay, that this seven-hundred-square-foot house wasn't vacant after all. It was an active drug den with addicts stopping by at all hours to buy and use narcotics. More than one neighbor was heard to say, "That place just needs to be torn down." It had no water or electricity; the utilities had not been turned on *for seven years*, we learned. The first time I walked through the place, the smell was overpowering. The one and only toilet was heaping with unflushed feces. I saw stacks of hypodermic needles and spoons for cooking drugs everywhere. On the walls in random places were little flaps of cloth; as I lifted them I discovered half-inch peepholes that had been drilled through the exterior brick by meth addicts, who tend to be ultra-paranoid.

We would have to gut the entire place and start over.

We prepped our work crew that hot Monday morning with gloves and respiratory masks as they began carrying everything they could out to a Dumpster. My older two sons—teenagers—were part of the team. It was a teachable moment for them about what the Bible means when it says, "The wages of sin is death."[1] I didn't have to say anything. The lie of society's fascination with drugs was obvious.

At one point I turned around on the front sidewalk, and there stood Breck.

"Hey, what's up?" I said, glad to see her again. Right away I noticed her somber expression. She wasn't nearly as upbeat as we'd always known her to be. Now she began to cry and was soon laying her head on my chest.

I let her just rest for a moment. Then she wiped her eyes with the back of her hand and got a resolute look on her face as she declared: "I need to help with this!"

Sure, okay.

She continued, "Pastor Matt, the reason I haven't been coming to church is because I can't stand the look of this house. It brings back memories that are just awful. I lay on the cold concrete floor of the basement for the better part of a year with a needle in my arm. This house was hell to me."

I was speechless. So I just kept quiet and waited.

"Whenever I came to church, I would go into an anxiety attack just being anywhere near this house. That's why you probably noticed me getting up and leaving in the middle of the service. I just had to get out of there."

I was amazed.

"The decisions of my life that still keep me up at night were made in this house," she continued. "Now I want to help with the demo. What can I do?"

Attack Mode

We gave her a mask and a sledgehammer. This little five-foot-three-inch force marched up the steps and started whaling away with a vengeance. Drywall chunks were flying everywhere as she vented her rage. She was a tigress on a rampage for the next hour and a half, until she completely wore herself out. It was the best psychotherapy she could ever have undertaken.

For the entire week she kept working with the team until every interior wall and fixture was gone. At times she would start crying again, but she wouldn't quit working. She wanted to see this pit of devastation completely smashed and turned into something good.

During breaks, the two of us would stand outside talking about grace and forgiveness. We talked about her need to forgive herself. I said, "You know, what's happening to this house is sort of a picture of what God is doing in your life." I mentioned that wonderful line from Joseph in the Old Testament, where he told his once-jealous brothers, "You intended to harm me, but God intended it for good to accomplish what is now being done, the saving of many lives."[2] I talked about how this house was soon going to be filled with guys getting their lives on track, free of the bondage of drugs.

At the end of every Wanna Give Away week, we have a Friday night celebration dinner. We tell stories from the week's work and encourage each other.

That week, Breck was finally ready to talk publicly. "I want to share," she told me. She got up in front of three hundred people and spilled her story, the whole nine yards.

Every time she would start to break down, the others would cheer her on. "You're all right, girl! Come on! It's all good—you're here now!" And they would clap until she got her bearings to continue.

This week had been a turning point for her. She had released the condemnation of her past. She had finally slain the dragon that tormented her. Her sunny disposition returned. She was now free in Christ to become the person God had made her to be.

Stories Are Essential

People have a deep longing to be accepted and loved for who they are, with all their baggage and failures. When they get up the courage to put it all out on the table, and our response is empathy and genuine love, we have created space for new beginnings to blossom. We've opened the door for them to believe that their broken life is not too bad for Jesus.

No two stories are ever the same. We hear a lot of them at the Genesis Project, and if we're ever tempted to toss any of them into the "general addict" file, we quickly stop. Each one has its uniqueness, its individuality. The more we listen, the more we're reminded of our desperate need for a *personal* Savior.

If churches don't make time, in the midst of all the formulas and programming and meetings and sermons and

> People have a deep longing to be accepted and loved for who they are, with all their baggage and failures.

committee meetings, to hear—really hear—personal stories, they miss a core element. Stories are living expressions of who people are—complex and simple, inspiring and frustrating, beautiful and catastrophic. Yes, some people's stories bog down in minutiae. But we must not let that irritate us. We must, in Jesus' memorable phrase, have "ears to hear."[3]

When you understand a person's story, it usually becomes a catalyst to see them differently. All the judgment drains out of you as you grasp what has turned them into the person they are.

It does no good to look at someone's *behavior* and turn it into their *identity*, a label on their forehead that reads "Addict" or "Wife Beater" or "Stripper" or "Philanderer." No . . . this is Linda or Jeff or Michelle or Danny. Real people with real histories.

To be honest, the two of us are not great fans of the traditional method of introducing oneself to a recovery group by saying, "My name is David and I'm an alcoholic" (or whatever the vice may be). It seems to reinforce the belief of "once an addict, always an addict."

> **You are a man, a woman, made in the image of God. He created you for a purpose. He loves you, and so do we. Together with him, you can get back to your true purpose.**

No. You are a man, a woman, made in the image of God. He created you for a purpose. He loves you, and so do we. Together with him, you can get back to your true purpose.

The moment any Christian thinks a broken person is unredeemable and unlovable . . . *stop*. Sit down and ask that person about his or her story. This will back you way off the ledge of condemnation.

Henry Wadsworth Longfellow, the great American poet of the 1800s, said wisely, "If we could read the secret history of our enemies, we should find in each man's life sorrow and suffering enough to disarm all hostility."[4] How very true.

When you value and respect a person's story, you actually value and respect the person. That is not to say you respect everything they've done. But you acknowledge the facts of their winding, twisting journey and what it has done to them.

Hiding Doesn't Help

If, however, a person's story is met with revulsion, shock, or judgmentalism, the door to wholeness will be slammed shut. The eminent Presbyterian pastor and speaker Bruce Larson, perhaps best known for such books as *Living Beyond Our Fears* and *There's a Lot More to Health Than Not Being Sick*, once told about a formative moment in his early ministry:

> I was a student minister at a little church up on the Hudson River—I'd go up every weekend from Princeton, where I was in seminary. I met my wife in that church, in fact. "Fellowship" consisted of a monthly meeting of the women's association and an occasional men's breakfast, where you had a baseball or football player come in and give his testimony.
>
> Then one weekend, I found out some shocking news: a teenage girl in the congregation had left town to go to her older brother's. She was pregnant. I said to the dear woman who told me, "Could I go and see her?"
>
> "Oh, no," she replied. "You're the *last* person she wants to know what happened."

Suddenly it hit me: *That's what's wrong with the church in our time.* It's the place you go when you put on your best clothes; you sit in Sunday school, you worship, you have a potluck dinner together—*but you don't bring your life!* You leave behind all your pain, your brokenness, your hopes, even your joys.

Larson then went on to acknowledge some improvement:

I think in almost any church of any size there are now at least some people trying to be real, asking "What does it mean for me to belong to Jesus Christ and also to belong to his family?"[5]

We certainly hope so! As long as people are discouraged from lifting the lid off what's really going on in their lives, progress is at a standstill. The epistle of James says, "Confess your sins to each other and pray for each other so that you may be healed. The prayer of a righteous person is powerful and effective."[6]

The minute we bring up the word *confession*, many Protestants are prone to object, "Oh, that's something the Catholics do." But, in fact, confession is the road to ultimate freedom. It defeats shame. It's not easy for either the one speaking or for those listening, but it can result, as James said, in coming to a place where "you may be healed."

I (Matt) once had a man sit in my office and own up to a shocking sex act—at which point his stunned wife, sitting beside him, began to retch and then throw up all over my desk. They had supposedly come to see me for marital counseling. Now everything had exploded into the open.

The rest of that situation was rough, indeed, as you can imagine. They ended up divorcing. She was so very angry, and he was so very ashamed of himself. I was not able to bring reconciliation to that union although she has continued to try to follow the Lord. Time will tell whether he can be touched by the hand of grace that refuses to see his sin as any worse than yours or mine.

Conviction Versus Condemnation

In every case, whether modest or extreme, we must recognize the difference between *conviction* and *condemnation*. Yes, the Holy Spirit brings conviction into the human heart that has sinned. That is part of his role, Jesus said.[7] He doesn't gloss over people's failings. He steers them to confess and move on.

He is a bit like Mick, the grizzled boxing coach in the old *Rocky* movies: "Come on, Rocky! Get up! Get back in there—you can do better!"

Condemnation, on the other hand, is the voice of Satan saying, "You're no good. You're worthless. You really messed up this time. Don't even bother trying anymore. If respectable people knew your secrets, they'd never speak to you again."

Confession—telling the story—is part of what silences the voice of condemnation. The more we in the church welcome the stories of troubled people, letting them get it out into the open, the more we move them forward. Otherwise, ugliness festers in the darkness.

I (Matt) still remember a middle-aged couple who came to me one Sunday afternoon quite disturbed. "This morning in church," they began, "we couldn't

> In every case, whether modest or extreme, we must recognize the difference between *conviction* and *condemnation*.

help noticing a lesbian couple sitting in the row right in front of us. All while you were speaking, they were holding hands and patting each other—it was disgusting.

"And then when it came time for Communion, they had the gall to stand up and get in line to receive the elements! We couldn't believe it.

"Something like this just has to be stopped. In fact, we'd like to head up a team that would monitor the Communion table to make sure people like this don't partake. It's for their own protection, of course. Doesn't the Bible say something about not eating the bread or drinking the cup 'unworthily'?[8] This just can't go on in our church."

I took a deep breath, then answered, "You know, you're right—something needs to be done. Here's what I foresee. How about if you guys come back next Sunday, find the two young ladies you sat behind, and invite them over to the coffee shop to chat? Sit down with them and ask to hear their story. See what it was like for them growing up. Find out how they came to be with each other. Ask them what's been drawing them to this church. Try to hear what's going on in their hearts.

"Then come back to me with what you've discovered. That will help me figure out where to go next."

The husband and wife rolled their eyes and stormed out of my office in a huff. I never saw them again.

Meanwhile, the couple in question has become a part of our church family. I've gotten to know some of their story, the complexity of their past, and their deep regard for each other. Together, they are raising children who are now a vibrant part of our kids' ministry.

After about a year of attending, the two women asked for an appointment with me. As soon as they sat down, one of them started weeping. "We love this church," she said through her tears. "It's so good for us and for the kids. But . . . we need to know something. Are you anti–our family? Are you against us? I'm terrified to ask."

"Why would I be anti-you?" I said.

"Well, because we're gay."

I tried to choose my words carefully. "You know what? We can sit here today and talk about a lot of perfect standards—and if we do, all three of us will leave this room feeling very inadequate. The truth is, my goal is to introduce you to a vibrant, intimate living relationship with Jesus. Because he's the only one with answers to the toughest questions.

"The biggest thing for all of us—you, me, everybody—is to ask whether we're really willing to respond to what Jesus asks of us. To make him the Lord of our lives. What I've learned over the years is that I can easily say those words, but the harder part is being willing to let go and trust him."

I made some more points, eventually leading up to the question "Is this the kind of relationship you want with Jesus?"

The first woman, still crying, nodded yes. The second woman looked me straight in the eye and said, "No."

"Tell me why," I gently persisted.

"Because he's going to ask me for my family, and I'm not willing to give it to him."

"Okay, that's honest," I replied. "The truth is, I don't have any easy answers for you today, but what if we keep meeting together and continue this conversation?"

And so the process continues to this day.

Hard to Hear

For those of us who are parents, our kids have stories too, especially our adult kids. How willing are we to hear and value their stories? This can be much harder because, the truth is, we parents are a part of that story whether for good or for bad—or for most of us, some of both.

In the Cowles and Roberts households, our kids have grown up as PKs (preacher's kids), a role that can carry tremendous pressure. The expectations placed on a pastor's family are often completely unrealistic.

I (Rob) will never forget the day my oldest son told me that what he learned most from the church was how to be a hypocrite. Those were difficult words to hear. But the question was, would I listen to and value *his* story? Sometimes we have all the time and grace in the world for someone else's story of brokenness, but we won't do the same for our own sons or daughters. And sometimes the reason we struggle is because we need to own a part of their story. I had to own that I had contributed to my son's perception that church, in general, championed hypocrisy over authenticity.

There's nothing worse than seeing our kids struggle and suffer. It can be especially hard when it's a result of poor decisions they're making, patterns they keep repeating, addictions that have made them slaves. And whether there's something for us parents to "own" in their story or not, what they need from us is not another lecture, another guilt trip, another bribe. What they need is for us to genuinely listen to their story and value their journey.

In spite of a parent's disappointment and hurt, kids need to know they're loved and valued. No matter what has happened, no matter what mistakes have been made, jobs lost, indictments pending . . . love endures.

Jesus' story about the prodigal son shows a dad waiting patiently day after day for his wayward boy to "[come] to his senses."⁹ He didn't send detectives to chase him down in the far country, although the father could certainly have afforded to hire them. He didn't write scathing or manipulative letters. He just kept waiting, looking down the long driveway . . . until the young man had hit bottom and chosen to seek a better life.

And suddenly, it was party time!

Often hitting bottom is what drives a person to rethink their life. But that's a hard prayer to pray when you're a parent: that your son or daughter, whom you love deeply, would hit bottom. Romans 2:4 tells us that it is God's kindness that leads us to repentance. What if you committed to pray every day for that one you love who has taken a destructive path, that God would overwhelm them with his kindness and that it would be undeniable to them that it came from him?

Don't Try This Alone

Sometimes we all struggle with the reality of a process. We like finish lines. Nothing is more satisfying than checking a "completed" box on a checklist.

But very rarely does the sacred space of walking in someone else's story afford us these neat and tidy boundaries.

Once we understand this, we begin to see everyone's story as the perfect place for a Savior to write his love story, instead of a mistake that needs our correcting. Opening up a person's story is a sacred trust and comes with great responsibility. Making excursions into the brokenness of someone's life so we can correct a mistake is, at best, ineffective and, at worst, detrimental.

Kindness and empathy are important traits for all of us as we listen to the stories of people. It allows the person to be honest and open the window for fresh air, fresh perspective.

Meanwhile, the longer we listen, the more we come to realize how utterly dependent on Jesus and his life-changing power we are. We don't have the answers in ourselves. Whatever textbooks we may have read will fall short. If Jesus doesn't show up in this person's life, there truly is no hope. We must take the attitude of Moses, who said to God at one point, "If your Presence does not go with us, do not send us up from here."[10]

We're not smart enough to map out any path of solution or healing on our own. We desperately need his guidance.

The messy stories are a starting point. Thank God they're not the end.

> The longer we listen, the more we come to realize how utterly dependent on Jesus and his life-changing power we are. We don't have the answers in ourselves.

5

WE PULL TOGETHER
SAFE COMMUNITIES

Dedria Johnson is a tall, no-nonsense, say-it-like-it-is woman who learned from the age of eight to fend for herself because no one else was going to help her survive. Born in New York City to a promiscuous, drug-addicted teenager, she lived with her maternal grandmother. Dedria's mom continued to have children and then pass them off to Dedria's grandmother to raise. But the elderly woman was battling cancer, and when she died, the kids were shoved into foster care.

"At that point my life became a living hell of physical and emotional abuse," she tells. "Molestation and rape were my reality. As a child, I didn't understand. I just tried to survive—for the next thirty-five years."

Like her mother, Dedria began having children at sixteen. Drugs and alcohol became daily escapes for her. Finally, she decided she and her family could use a fresh start. They headed west for Colorado.

"The trouble was, I brought all my old 'stuff' with me," she admits. Eventually in 2015, the household (which by now included three grandchildren) became homeless—which is how they showed up at the Genesis Project thanks to Fort Collins's FFH (see chapter 3) program. This tough, independent-minded woman from the big city needed help.

Our congregation was fairly new to the work of hosting a family in our building for a week. We welcomed them as best we knew how, tried to make them comfortable, smiled a lot, and engaged in conversation. We fell in love with her darling kids and grandkids.

Dedria told us later, "From the moment we walked in, I felt more at home than any place I'd ever lived. You allowed my soul to flourish. It all reminded me of the warmth I had felt as a little girl back in my grandmother's church before she died. I knew that what I needed most was to come back to God."

Soon after the week was up, we helped her get into an apartment by providing the security deposit. One of her adult sons moved back in as well, helping to pay the rent. Dedria and her family started coming regularly to church. They began volunteering in any way they could. When our Friday night "Restore" ministry began, she joined right away, seeking to get honest about her tendencies.

Then came the day she said to me, "I want to be baptized." Relatives from back East flew in for the occasion. Her testimony that day concluded, "I thank God for what he's doing in my life. I've done everything else; now all I want is to be more like Jesus. I've found the love I was looking for, and he has my heart forever."

When she came up out of the water, the place exploded into the most joyous celebration you could imagine.

She had arrived at a place to belong, a place perhaps best described as *safe*.

On the Hunt

Nearly everyone in a troubled state has felt the sting of fake or faux community. In their minds they keep wondering, *Where can I connect with people who won't take advantage of me, rip me off, embarrass me?*

Millennials these days talk about wanting what they call a "third space" (in addition to their apartment and their workplace), where they can find others on safe terrain. They want to feel at ease, unthreatened. They crave more than just one hundred or five hundred Facebook friends.

Isn't this what Jesus always meant the church to be? Wasn't this the "secret sauce" of the early church—a place that transcended Jew or Gentile, rich or poor, young or old, educated or illiterate?

God calls his followers to refuse the dualistic mind-set of us versus them, the mainstream saints versus the needy sinners. Galatians 5:26 says it well in *The Message* paraphrase: "We will not compare ourselves with each other as if one of us were better and another worse. We have far more interesting things to do with our lives. Each of us is an original."

Nearly everyone in a troubled state has felt the sting of fake or faux community. In their minds they keep wondering, *Where can I connect with people who won't take advantage of me, rip me off, embarrass me?*

All of us are in need of rescue on a journey to become what God envisions for our lives. And we do that better together than alone. Community is like a garden trellis that allows the wisteria and the honeysuckles of organic relationship to blossom and steadily grow upward.

Too many of us grew up in church cultures where the accepted sequence for newcomers was

1. *Believe* (the gospel, i.e., become saved), then
2. *Behave* (clean up your life) so finally you can
3. *Belong* (enter the corporate fellowship of the body).

At the Genesis Project we've changed the order. Our pattern is

1. *Belong*, then
2. *Believe*, and, as a result,
3. *Behave*.

Granted, it's a lot messier this way. Church is harder to manage; in fact, it's impossible to control. But the new person is not made to feel that he must believe all the right doctrines and clean up his act before he'll be welcomed into the spiritual community. We find that the context of community is often where people come to believe new truths and change old ways.

The main invitation is not just "come to church." It is rather an invitation into a living organism—a place of belonging not defined by a specific time or space. Church is not a place we go but the lives we live. We *do life* together. No matter where you come from, what you've been through, or how scrambled your current circumstances, this is a team sport, and it's safe for you to be a part of this team.

Stop and think about the fruit of the Holy Spirit listed in Galatians 5:22–23. It is very *communal*. You can't demonstrate patience or kindness if you're keeping to yourself. There's no way to show love or gentleness if you're living on an island. These qualities get put into play only in the context of community.

But It's Not Easy

We need to be honest, though, and admit that healthy, safe community is not natural to a fallen world. Human beings have a tendency to gravitate toward cliques, to pull off toward people like themselves, to go back to *us* and *them*. There's a reason the apostle Paul told the Ephesian believers to "*make every effort* to keep the unity of the Spirit."[1] Another translation puts it bluntly: "*Work hard* to live together as one by the help of the Holy Spirit."[2] It takes work, for sure.

While people such as Dedria may find a church like the Genesis Project to be welcoming and safe, others sometimes actually call it *unsafe*. They're not sure they want to be (or want their kids to be) around such sketchy personalities. The two of us have had more than a few conversations with people that go like this:

"Hey, I haven't seen you guys recently. How are you doing?"

"Oh, well, we've been going to another church."

"Okay, that's fine. You're still following Jesus. But just for my benefit, give me some feedback about the Genesis Project. I'd love to hear what you're thinking."

"Well . . . it just seems like you guys mainly focus on drug addicts and people in recovery and so forth. It's just not the kind of church we're looking for. We need to be in a church with people like us."

In such moments what we pastors *want* to say (but try to restrain ourselves!) is, "Well, you're going to hate being in heaven. Because it's going to include tons of broken people who've been redeemed."

Jesus was a renegade against the buttoned-up religious culture of his day. He had this thing about rubbing shoulders with the marginalized, the down-and-out, the disreputable. So did Paul, a well-educated Pharisee whom God turned into a missionary to the Gentiles. That's why he could write to the Roman believers: "Do not be proud, but be willing to associate with people of low position. Do not be conceited."[3]

The truth is, successful people can be as broken as meth addicts. They just know how to hide it better.

Two Slippery Slopes

Any community trying to be safe and redemptive is at risk from two gravitational forces, tugging from opposite sides.

The first, to which we've already alluded, is to be *law-dominant*, to exalt the laws of God above all else. Church folks call it "standing for righteousness" or "holding the standard." After all, the reasoning goes, if the church doesn't model what purity means, nobody else is going to.

The two of us meet people all the time who got wounded long ago by a church somewhere and walked away. For them, God was perceived as the Big Cop in the Sky, enforcing rules and regulations. These people knew they didn't match up and figured they never could. Now they're afraid to reveal the ugliness that festers inside.

One mean-spirited person in a congregation can derail the

> The truth is, successful people can be as broken as meth addicts. They just know how to hide it better.

atmosphere of safety. One Facebook post about what somebody revealed in a recovery group can send a chill through the entire community. We will directly confront such a person, saying, "You do not have permission to air other people's dirty laundry, even indirectly or as a 'prayer request.' That's not what it means to be a safe community. Can you abide by that? If not, we will be glad to help you find a different church." (And, in fact, we've done so on a few occasions.)

The second force, however, is to become *sin-tolerant*, as in, "Yeah, we're all broken, and that's just the way it is, but we want to be sure everybody feels good about themselves."

I (Matt) talked with one guy who had been going to an SA (Sexaholics Anonymous) group. How was he told to cope with his addiction? Use pornography and masturbation instead, they said. He told me, "When I heard that, something inside me just knew that wasn't right." No, it wasn't.

Some Christians today can claim that they don't do drugs, but, meanwhile, they're hedonistic in every other sense. They diligently avoid three or four infamous sins while blithely indulging in six or seven others that Scripture clearly condemns. To maintain a safe community does not mean we don't confront one another in love. It's actually a demonstration of caring when we say to a fellow believer, "I love you enough to bring up a sticky subject with you. Can we have an honest conversation about _____?"

In between the two extremes of law-dominance and sin-tolerance is, thankfully, a middle zone called *grace*. It recognizes that sin certainly matters but also that forgiveness is available, and change is possible. God loves us in our weakness, but he loves us too much to let us stay there. He wants to lift us to a higher plane.

Maintaining a healthy, safe community is not about wobbling

back and forth, in one moment toward law, in the next toward tolerance. Neither of these would please the One who called us. It takes great effort for any church, any class, any small group, or any individual Christian to stay centered and balanced upon the simple and incredible truth of God's love and grace. It is this truth that compels us to live different lives.

A Laboratory for Change

Jesus gave us a laboratory for working out the gospel in messy, disordered lives. It's called the Christian community. And in order for it to be effective, it has to be a safe place.

We see that particularly in our recovery groups, which we call "Recovery in Christ." That name is intentional, in that the starting point as each group convenes is not "how's everybody feeling tonight?" or "who's battling which addiction?" It is, rather, *our identity in Christ. Who does he say we are?*

Identity is the seed of every other choice we make in life. Our first task, therefore, is to establish identity in faith. Outside of that, the group ministry really doesn't have much to offer. We're a one-trick pony! We have only one answer, and that is Jesus.

The story of the gospel is not behavior modification. Jesus didn't die to modify your behavior or mine. He died to pay for our sins and bring us into a whole new life.

The groups, therefore, are not a program from which people graduate after ten

> Jesus gave us a laboratory for working out the gospel in messy, disordered lives. It's called the Christian community.

or twelve weeks. The point is to assimilate into the life of the larger church. We don't think in terms of *recovery* people and *regular* people. We're all just people coming closer and closer to Jesus, who is the only one who can fix our brokenness. Therein lies safety for every person who's worried about fitting in.

If it is true that genuine, safe relationships are the most effective conduits through which the gospel can travel, then within the borders of community, we obviously need to cultivate them, not squelch them. We don't have to get up on a soapbox regarding every social or behavioral issue. We don't have to answer questions other people aren't even asking. Instead, we need to rest in the knowledge that the Good Shepherd loves broken people more deeply than anyone else ever could, and will bring them to himself as we cooperate with him.

6

WE GET HONEST ABOUT SIN

Some readers may wonder whether, alongside all our talk about unconditional love and compassion and building safe communities, we would ever dare to whisper the S-word: *sin*. Should the broken people just be hugged and affirmed and welcomed without mentioning the errors that got them into their predicaments in the first place?

Not at all. The two of us talk about sin all the time—although not in the way (or with the tone) some might assume.

In fact, we often don't even have to initiate the topic; people who have messed up their lives do it on their own. They know deep inside how much they have strayed from a wise or godly path. They're beyond playing games or trying to whitewash their histories.

We think about Mike, a handsome, muscular biker in his early thirties who showed up at the Fort Collins coffee shop that first year before we had even gotten our actual building ready for use. He asked to meet with me (Rob). Within minutes he was admitting, "Man, I'm a sex addict. I bring home probably three different women a week." Pornography was not even an issue with Mike, because he could attract the real thing any night he wanted.

Tears ran down his face as he said, "My son came to me the other day. He's only twelve years old. He looked me square in the eye and said, 'You know what? As a dad, you suck.' I was devastated. I've got to change."

We got him into a yearlong program for sexual addiction. He showed up every week for his sessions. After graduation he ended up marrying the love of his life, the girlfriend who had left him years before because he couldn't seem to stay faithful. Today he runs a Bible study at their house for members of hard-core motorcycle clubs.

The general American culture would have smiled and even applauded a guy who could seduce that many women. He would have fit right in to any number of sitcoms. But Mike was miserable. He didn't try to tiptoe around his behavior with me; he wanted relief from the jabbing pain in his soul.

The Wages of Sin

The apostle's blunt statement in Romans 6:23, "The wages of sin is death," should not be viewed as some kind of religious scare tactic. It's true! It's about the most intuitive statement we can make. The broken person hears it and readily thinks, *Yeah . . . I know, all too well.*

My (Matt's) teenage sons have seen heroin addicts withdraw. They've heard guys high on meth frantically banging on our door at night trying to get ahold of me. They know what prostitutes look like because they've seen them walking into the Genesis Project. They get the fact that there's nothing cute about sin.

We've never, ever heard a drug addict say, "This is the life I've always wanted." We've never heard an alcoholic say, "I've never been happier." Instead, they recognize that something is seriously askew in their existence, taking them down a dreadful path.

Too many church kids grow up (as the two of us did) thinking that sin is an exhaustive list of things to be avoided because they will upset an already-angry God.

Once you get close to real people trapped in sin, you realize it's anything but a pretty life. It's a painful way to exist. It's something you want to escape, if at all possible, before it kills you.

Time and again we sit with people and say, "All this brokenness you're experiencing in your life is not the core problem; these are symptoms of something deeper called sin. The emotional pain, the disruption, the busted relationships, the lost jobs, the brushes with the law, the physical toll, the insecurities, the worries that keep you awake at night—these are just effects. The root cause is sin.

"And do you know what? It's okay for you and me, collectively, to hate what's killing us. There's nothing offensive about that. If a doctor says you have cancer, you don't get mad at him. You can blurt out, 'I hate cancer!' and he'll probably reply, 'So do I.'"

Some pastors say they don't want to preach about sin because they don't want to offend. Well . . . the wages of sin is death, regardless. If a physician tells you that your cancer is going to require surgery, and it's going to hurt, you say, "Okay, go ahead." You just want to get well.

> "The wages of sin is death" should not be viewed as some kind of religious scare tactic. It's true! The broken person hears it and readily thinks, *Yeah . . . I know, all too well.*

Sin is our common enemy. It robs, kills, and destroys. When a marriage falls apart, that's a symptomatic work of this enemy. When the abuse of prescription drugs gets out of hand, it's a sign of the one who wants to destroy us. Saying so is not a bad thing; it's simply stating the fact.

The Bible tells us that "grace *and truth* came through Jesus Christ."[1] Not just grace, which we all welcome. He also came to declare *truth*—the truth about ourselves, our self-destruction, and the remedy he offers so we can become the people he created us to be.

The Choice

Rarely a week goes by that we don't open our Bibles to Deuteronomy 30 and show someone what God said to the people of Israel:

> See, I set before you today life and prosperity, death and destruction. . . .
>
> This day I call the heavens and the earth as witnesses against you that I have set before you life and death, blessings and curses. Now choose life, so that you and your children may live and that you may love the LORD your God, listen to his voice, and hold fast to him. For the LORD is your life.[2]

We follow up by saying, "God loves you. He's your perfect Father. He doesn't want to see you hurting. He's giving you a choice.

"The part about calling the heavens and the earth as witnesses— it's the language of a courtroom. Heaven and earth are on the witness stand. What are they saying about you? What are the circumstances of your life declaring? Are they saying, 'This person keeps choosing death and destruction'?"

From this point we can move into a loving conversation about turning toward life and blessings.

More than seventy years ago a brilliant missionary evangelist to India named E. Stanley Jones wrote a devotional book simply titled *The Way*. He didn't focus so much on good versus evil or right versus wrong; instead, he took Jesus' famous statement of "I am the way"[3] and expanded it into a perspective on how all of life works out.

When God made you and me and the universe, He stamped within us a way. It is a part of us. . . . The way to live is not merely written in sacred books, but it is also written into our blood, our nerves, our tissues, our organs. It is not only written in texts of scriptures, but in the very texture of our beings. It is not imposed but exposed—exposed from our very make-up.[4]

This leads Jones to speak throughout his book about two roads we all can travel: "the Way" or "not-the-way." He gives a homely illustration from the world of science:

In chemistry, H_2O produces water. You may fight with the formula and try to twist it into something else, but in the end you will surrender to it, accept it, obey it—or you will not produce water. Two parts of hydrogen and one of oxygen is the way; and everything else is not the way. Chemistry did not invent this law or impose it; chemistry discovered it.[5]

The same is true, he says, in human activities and relationships. Some things are the way to live; others are simply not-the-way.

When we think about the sin, we should not think of a bunch of distasteful don'ts handed down by a grouchy, joy-killing God. We should rather admit that the very nature of our world gives us choices between things that are life-giving and things that are not-the-way.

But Wait!

Everything we've been saying up to this point, however, must not be dropped out of the sky onto a person. Truth must never be separated from a genuine, well-established relationship of caring and concern. Jesus was an active presence in the lives of drunks, tax collectors, and those called "sinners" by most other religious people. Within this engagement he was able to speak the truth honestly.

Relationship is like a bank account. Talking with someone about a sin issue represents a withdrawal from the account. But we have to make sure we have an adequate balance on hand to more than cover the withdrawal.

At the Genesis Project we often preface conversations by saying, "You know I love you, right? I really do care about you. And because I love you, can we have an honest conversation about _____?" That is what the Bible means when it talks about "speaking the truth in love."[6]

Relationship is the capital by which we can express the hardest of truths. Once we have proven a true love with no strings attached, we can speak hard truths.

If someone is in a pit, it doesn't do much good to holler down, "Hey! You need to get up out of that muck—up here, where I am!" They already know that much. What they need is for someone to lovingly get down next to them and help them figure out how to extract themselves, how to choose life instead of death.

Actually, we don't get down in the mud alone, trying to diagnose the intricacies of the person's misconduct; the Rescuer goes ahead of us. Jesus is, according to Scripture, "the pioneer and perfecter of faith."[7] He is the one who started this whole plan of redemption at the cross, and he's also the one who can execute the plan to perfection. He has written our whole story from start to glorious finish if we are willing to cooperate with him.

We sometimes ask people in distress, "Do you feel as if you're living the story God has written for your life?" Of course not, they admit. We're all in need of reclamation. None of us is fully what he intends us to be. And so it shouldn't surprise us that he wants to change some things in our muddied lives.

New Testament scholars tell us that the most frequent Greek word for *sin* is *hamartia*, to miss the mark. It's an archery term for not hitting the center of the target. Any sin in our lives is simply a case of living outside God's intent for us.

When we do this, we get "wages" (returning to the language of Romans 6:23). Our sinful behavior earns for us the result of death, in one or more of its various forms. It's not so much a matter of an angry God slapping us for what we did as it is the purely understandable payout for our deed. As E. Stanley Jones puts it, "To follow the Way brings results; not to follow brings consequences. . . . Apparently we are free to choose, but we are not free to choose the results of our choosing. Those results seem to be in hands not our own."[8]

Sorting all this out can be wonderfully enlightening, but it can succeed only in the context of the most essential element: real relationships. Otherwise, the words fall on deaf ears.

The Holy Spirit Goes to Work

Once a person—anybody—reaches up and out to Jesus, the Rescuer, the Holy Spirit goes to work. In our ministries, we are repeatedly amazed at how often a person comes up and says, "I just realized I need to make this change in my life," when we've never even addressed it. We never preached a sermon on that topic. The Spirit, instead, was working on them internally. He'd been quietly saying, *Here is truth— what are you going to do with it? Are you going to adjust your life or not?*

Christian psychologist and bestselling author Dr. Henry Cloud writes in his book *Necessary Endings* about the difference between the wise person and the foolish person. When truth comes to a wise person, they try to adjust their life to fit the truth. On the other hand, when truth comes to a foolish person, they often try to adjust the truth to fit their life.[9] Truth confronts us all constantly. What are we going to do with it?

Sometimes this confrontation can be jarring. In the Fort Collins church, one of the former strippers at the Hunt Club and her new husband, a former heroin addict, showed up and dramatically gave themselves to Jesus. They set their lives on a whole new course. They were enthusiastic to follow the Lord's path for their future.

One Easter we were busy doing an egg hunt for the children when, in the midst of kids running everywhere, the woman came up to our children's ministry director with a question. "Can I ask you something?"

"Okay," the director replied while simultaneously trying to keep an eye on the hubbub all around.

"My husband and I really want to do what pleases God. So is it wrong for us to have sex while watching porn?"

Our director (once she swallowed the gulp in her throat) said,

"Well, I guess I'd say that what you and your husband agree to do sexually is between the two of you—but pornography is dangerous, no matter what. It can seriously pollute your marriage. It isn't what God has in mind for your thoughts and imaginations." (I was quite proud of her for coming up with that much of an answer in the middle of an Easter egg hunt!)

If the woman had felt entirely comfortable with what she and her husband were doing, she would never have inquired about it. She didn't have any prior religious training or taboo nagging her. But something didn't feel quite right. She felt she'd better check it out.

The Christian term for what she was sensing is *conviction*. As we said back in chapter 4, this is not *condemnation*; this is, rather, the voice of God saying, *You can do better than this. I have a better way for you than where you're stuck just now.*

The One Solution

The Bible holds out just one solution for sin: *repentance.* Is that a distasteful word for modern ears to hear? It shouldn't be. It's one of the most beautiful, hopeful words in Scripture because it means *I don't have to stay like this. Through Jesus, I can turn in a completely different direction.*

People who are broken are not seeking a nice, soft message of "You're good, I'm good, we're all good. Let's just try to be a little better." They want someone to get in their face and challenge them.

Sin is not something you can counsel away. It's not something you can "modify." It's something you need to abandon straight-out—and Jesus can help you do it! That is really good news.

A lot of people in our society complain that life isn't fair:

"So-and-so has it in for me." "The system is against me." Well, actually, most of the unpleasant events that besiege us in life *are* fair, whether we like to admit it or not. Not all of them, to be sure—but in many cases we're getting the "wages" of what we've done, the bad harvest of the seeds we've sown.

There's little point in blaming others. Adam and Eve tried that way back in the garden of Eden. First, Adam blamed his wife. He even blamed God for giving him such a wife. Then she blamed the serpent. It did no good. People today still do this kind of weaving and dodging.

> **Sin is not something you can counsel away. It's not something you can "modify." It's something you need to abandon straight-out—and Jesus can help you do it!**

Do you want to know what is *really* unfair? The gospel! To receive a shot at cleansing our consciences and starting afresh is really amazing, thanks to the grace of God. Let's be honest: the last thing in the world we should ever want is what we deserve. How much better to choose grace.

Repentance is more than a onetime declaration. It is the deliberate choice to die to ourselves and surrender to Jesus as King. This is a choice we must make every day. Such was the case with Tara, a forty-something woman who started coming to our Ogden church five or six years ago. Living in a halfway house, she had done a major prison term for identity theft—her way of scraping up money to support her drug habit and way of life. Now she was clean and intent on starting a new life with the Lord.

The more we got to know Tara, the more we learned what an incredible woman she was. She knew a lot of the Bible from faithfully attending Bible studies and church services while in prison. She could quote Scripture verses with ease. She was "on fire" to follow the God who had rescued her from her former life. Her life of following Jesus was encouraging.

One day she shared with me, "My husband is getting out of prison soon. We need help. We have to figure out how we're going to go forward from here." I had never met her husband, but I knew that he had been incarcerated for the same kind of financial crimes as she.

Tara was eager for her husband to follow her to church. She would talk very openly about how God had changed her life, forgiven her sins, and put her on a better road. She could articulate forgiveness and restoration in eloquent and beautiful terms.

"Pastor Matt," she announced one day, "we want you to do a renewal of our wedding vows. That would be so great, now that we're following Jesus."

This gave me the opportunity to suggest that the three of us get together to do some marital counseling since they had been apart for so long. Those appointments let me know this couple even better as we discussed what makes a Christian marriage work well. The actual vow-renewal day was a joy to conduct.

But then . . . fast-forward about a year. Suddenly I got an urgent text from Tara: We need to talk to you ASAP!

The three of us sat down together, and the news came out that she'd had an affair with a coworker, she had lost her job as a result, and she was relapsing back into drugs. "I messed up!" she cried. "It's really bad."

"But now," she continued, turning to her husband, "he won't forgive me, and I don't even know if I can forgive myself!"

Her husband, meanwhile, sat with slumped shoulders, saying nothing. I could see tears in his eyes, but he wasn't about to speak up for his point of view.

Sin was making a strong comeback. I could see that Tara believed this was just "who they were." It was who they had been for so long that, from this vantage point, there didn't seem to be any hope for something different in sight. Tara knew all of the promises of God and was willing to believe them for everyone but herself.

"Let me ask you something, Tara. What if the tables were turned? What if Candice and I had come in here and told you guys everything you've just told me? How would that go down?"

"I couldn't even imagine that!" she replied.

"Well, then," I continued, "how dare you believe that God's best for anyone else's life would be any different than his best for you?"

Tara broke down. She saw herself in the mirror of what I had just described. She poured out her sincere sorrow to her husband for her actions and begged for his pardon. She asked God to pick her up once again and restore her by his grace. Repentance is truly a beautiful thing.

When we look at sin through the lens of the law, we become lawyers looking for loopholes. But when we look at sin for what it truly is, we realize it makes the heart of God mourn because he loves us so much. We hear in our minds the warning of Scripture, "If you think you are standing firm, be careful that you don't fall!"[10] We come to think about it the way he thinks. This opens the door for genuine healing and restoration.

Our Best Strategy

In the face of fallenness—whether the first time, the second time, or the twentieth time—what is the wisest response a Christian friend or leader can make? What will bring the best outcome?

Our mutual friend Dick Foth tells about a time of frustration when, as a young pastor trying to launch a church in Urbana, Illinois, he was complaining to God about people's shortcomings. They just weren't living the way Dick knew would be best for their lives.

In that time of prayer, he sensed God saying to him, *Why don't you stop telling people what to do and start telling them who I am? And then let* me *tell them what to do.*

This changed his whole approach to ministry, not only in that church but in his subsequent responsibilities as a college president and then as a special envoy for Christ among government officials in Washington, DC. His focus on the gracious love of God to overcome all our human failings won a hearing wherever he went.

Our role is to lift up the ne who shows a better way.

When Jesus stood over the woman caught in the act of adultery, he didn't say, "Okay, now let's recap what your sin is." His most memorable line, in fact, was "Neither do I condemn you.... Go now and leave your life of sin."[11] He could tell she already felt the weight of conviction. What she needed most was his forgiveness.

The Deception of Sin

The Devil never stops trying to convince us that our way is better than God's. This has been the lie of sin from the very beginning.

Søren Kierkegaard, the nineteenth-century Danish philosopher and theologian, wrote a witty parable about the greatest jewel heist in history. Some thieves broke into a store one night. They didn't steal anything; they just began switching price tags so that the cheap stuff now carried the high-end tags while the truly valuable items had low prices. The next day they returned to buy valuable necklaces and other jewelry at bargain rates.

Satan has a way of confusing our value estimations. He makes the cheap things of this world seem priceless. People end up paying the highest price for a lie.

Eventually we all must come to agree with what King Solomon wrote long ago in the book of Ecclesiastes: sin is a dead-end street, "a chasing after the wind" (he uses the phrase nine times).[12] Here was a man who had slept with just about every woman he could find. "I denied myself nothing my eyes desired; I refused my heart no pleasure," he declared. Yet "everything was meaningless... nothing was gained."[13]

You can hear the wind, can feel it blowing on your skin; sometimes you can even smell its aroma. It fools your senses into thinking you're getting closer, closer. But you'll never chase it down. You wind up empty-handed, disappointed. That's how it is with sin.

At the end of the day, after a person has owned up to his brokenness and heard about the gracious escape that Jesus offers, he—and he alone—has to decide whether to repent or not. We can't stitch this onto his shirt from the outside. It's up to him to make the decision.

When Jesus talked with the rich young ruler and finished reviewing what a good fellow he had been all his life, he then zeroed in on the man's one problem: his materialism. He cut right to the chase by asking him to give it all away, then to come and follow the true Master. The guy couldn't pull that switch. "When the young man heard this, he went away sad, because he had great wealth."[14]

Jesus did not chase after him. He didn't call out, "Wait a minute! Let's keep talking. How about giving away just half? Whaddya think?" Instead, he let him walk.

Those are hard moments in the life of anyone trying to reach sin-trapped people. You want so badly for them to come to repentance and the freedom that follows. But after all your loving explanations, you can't put words in their mouths. Only they can decide to "choose life."

7

WE EXTEND GOD'S
FORGIVENESS AND FREEDOM

Author Ernest Hemingway held a special affinity for the country of Spain. Some say his best novel is *For Whom the Bell Tolls*, set in the Spanish Civil War of the late 1930s, which Hemingway covered as a reporter for the North American Newspaper Alliance. At the beginning of one of his short stories, he briefly mentions a tale circulating in the capital city:

> Madrid is full of boys named Paco, which is the diminutive of the name Francisco, and there is a Madrid joke about a father who came to Madrid and inserted an advertisement in the personal columns of *El Liberal* which said: PACO MEET ME AT HOTEL MONTANA NOON TUESDAY ALL IS FORGIVEN PAPA and how a squadron of Guardia Civil had to be called out to disperse the eight hundred young men who answered the advertisement.[1]

Whether the story was true or apocryphal, it shows the deep human longing for pardon. Go anywhere in the world, talk to anyone, young or old, and if you can get them to be honest, you will find them wishing their slate could be wiped clean, their offenses forgiven, their brokenness healed. If only they could close the chapter on what they did. If only they could be restored to their loved ones. If only their accusing memories could be melted away.

Therein lies *freedom*—a huge release from the regrets of the past. It is actually even more than that. Freedom is being able to live in the wide-open spaces of God's grace and mercy. It is becoming fully human, the state God intended for us all. As Paul puts it, "It is for freedom that Christ has set us free. Stand firm, then, and do not let yourselves be burdened again by a yoke of slavery."[2]

But when you know you've done despicable things—when you've admitted your very real sins and mistakes—freedom maybe sounds like a pipe dream. Could you be granted a reset, a do-over? Could God redeem your mess?

Man in the Shadows

One of the most poignant Old Testament stories is that of David reaching out to the crippled, marginalized, forgotten grandson of the previous monarch, King Saul. His name was a mouthful: Mephibosheth (*muh-FIB-uh-sheth*). His life had been tragic from the time when he was just five years old. The enemy army of the Philistines had overrun his grandfather in battle, his brave father (Jonathan) had also been killed that day, and the panicky nurse who grabbed the little boy to flee for safety ended up dropping him as she ran, wrecking grave fractures to his feet.[3] He never walked normally again.

When in 2 Samuel 9 we meet him years later as a grown man, he is living in somebody else's house in a dusty, out-of-the-way village on the far side of the Jordan River called Lo Debar. The name pretty much says it all; in Hebrew it means "no pasture." Was Mephibosheth trying to stay incognito? Clearly he knew that whenever a regime change happened in those times, it was normal practice to kill off all the heirs of the deposed king. That way no one from the old dynasty could try to retake the throne.

Was his name still on a long-delayed hit list somewhere? Maybe the current king would just keep ignoring him, letting him live out his years in obscurity.

One day royal messengers from Jerusalem came riding into the little village. Finding Mephibosheth, they said King David had hunted him down and wanted to see him. He should pack a bag and come with them immediately. Scripture doesn't tell us whether or not his heart began racing in that moment. Had his time finally come?

As it turned out, he arrived in the court of the king to hear these soothing words: "Don't be afraid . . . for I will surely show you kindness for the sake of your father Jonathan. I will restore to you all the land that belonged to your grandfather Saul."[4] The little man on crutches could hardly believe his ears.

But the king wasn't done. He wasn't just going to put on a nice dinner that evening and then send Mephibosheth home again the next morning. The king was thinking long term as he added, "And you will always eat at my table." Unbelievable!

> In every nation, no matter how wealthy, there are pockets of broken, hurting, marginalized, discarded people who have been stuffed out of sight.

What this story says to us is that God our King cares about places like Lo Debar. In every nation, no matter how wealthy, there are pockets of broken, hurting, marginalized, discarded people who have been stuffed out of sight. Some of them would admit to making stupid mistakes they now regret; others, like Mephibosheth, got dropped by another person who should have protected them. Whatever the history, they're now passing their days in hopelessness.

But the King of kings sees all, and he cares enough to send his servants to look for them. He gives a commission that runs something like this: *Go find those who are afraid of me because they don't know my heart. They think I take delight in punishment, not forgiveness. I want to talk to them, to lift up their heads, to restore their dignity, to give them a bright future.*

Three times in the story David uses the word *kindness* (vv. 1, 3, 7). The Hebrew word is *hesed*, which carries a much richer meaning than our English equivalent. We think we're being kind when we hold open the door for somebody in a wheelchair. The Hebrew word connotes something much deeper: the life-sustaining grace of God.

He is the God who invites broken people to sit at the family table alongside princes and princesses—*permanently*. Is not this the heart of the gospel? Those who have been wounded, who carry shame, who've been shoved to the edges of society . . . the King is sending messengers their way. How beautiful is that?

For Real?

Time and again we say to broken people that God invites us all into the center of his kingdom, not to be exploited as peasants but to be adopted as family members, clean and forgiven of all our past.

When people truly hear this, you can almost see their emotions swell. Right during a sermon, tears start welling up in their eyes. They've never imagined they could be forgiven or restored. Shame has beaten them down, destroyed their spirit . . . and now they see a God who knows all their junk and loves them anyway.

These people think (and sometimes even say to us), "Are you sure about this? I mean, how could God just forgive me? After all the stuff I've done? Seriously?"

Yes, it's true.

At the Genesis Project it is common for us to have two or three registered sex offenders attending at any one time. We don't announce this publicly, of course. But we've met with their probation officers, when necessary, and have set safety protocols in place.

But let's all face the question: Do we believe what the Bible says about God's grace to forgive or not? Is any sin—even against a child—beyond the circle of his love? The apostle Paul said he had been "the worst of sinners," needing "Christ Jesus [to] display his immense patience as an example for those who would believe in him and receive eternal life."[5] If a drug addict, wife beater, murderer (like Paul), or topless dancer can't come to church and hear the good news, where else can he or she go?

Forgiveness is God's zero point on the continuum that heads toward new life.

Jesus' parable about the prodigal son shows the heart of our heavenly Father in vivid colors. The obnoxious kid had done everything wrong, starting when he asked for his half of the estate. That

> **If a drug addict, wife beater, murderer (like Paul), or topless dancer can't come to church and hear the good news, where else can he or she go?**

was equivalent, in that culture, to blurting, "I wish you were dead already!" Then he went out and proceeded to blow his father's hard-earned cash on ridiculous things. Eventually he ran out of money, hit bottom, and had to work as a pig feeder (particularly disgusting to a Jewish boy) until he found no choice but to return to his home.

He made up a speech. He knew he didn't deserve to be considered a son again. But maybe he could be a hired hand, out in the fields or taking care of cattle. *It's worth a shot*, he thought to himself.

Meanwhile, what was the father thinking? Had he written off this kid as an ungrateful, no-good rogue?

Picture the man in the afternoon shadows, peering down the long driveway. Will his son ever show up again? If so, in what shape?

"While he was still a long way off, his father saw him and was filled with compassion for him; he ran to his [barefoot] son, threw his arms around him and kissed him." The son started into his little speech, but didn't even get to the let-me-be-a-servant bit before his father interrupted, "Quick! Bring the best robe and put it on him. Put a ring on his finger and sandals on his feet. Bring the fattened calf and kill it. Let's have a feast and celebrate."[6]

That's what God-minded parents (and friends and churches) do. They surround the repentant person with hugs and love and cheers. They don't know for sure if this change will "stick" long term, but they don't even want to talk about it. They are too busy rejoicing.

Somebody asked me (Matt) once, "Are you guys a church that preaches cheap grace?"

Yep. The threshold for receiving God's forgiveness is incredibly low. He has seen all our human stupidity; nothing has shocked him up to this point. Now he just wants to get on with restoration. As soon as any of us expresses our sorrow and desire to walk a new direction, he's on it! "I, even I, am he who blots out your transgressions, for my own sake, and remembers your sins no more."[7] If we were to ask him, "Yeah, but what about that thing I did four or six or ten years ago?" he would reply in all truthfulness, "I don't know what you're talking about."

The Battle Within

But some people say, "The trouble is, I could never forgive myself." They may accept (at least theologically) that a loving God could forgive their wicked deeds, but inside their own head, it's another story. They're so filled with shame and regret that they feel permanently unworthy.

Dr. Richard Dobbins, a pastor and then the founder of a counseling ministry in Akron, Ohio, once told about a forty-something woman named Evelyn who came to see him, saying, "There's something I need to talk to you about— but I'm afraid if you know, you'll never have any respect for me." It took several sessions before she finally revealed that as a teenager, she and her boyfriend had gotten pregnant. The church of which they were a part had handled the situation badly, humiliating them both.

> He has seen all our human stupidity; nothing has shocked him up to this point. Now he just wants to get on with restoration.

They went ahead and got married—but, Dr. Dobbins recalled, "she wasn't sure whether he had married her because he loved her or because he had to. He had told her a hundred times or more that he had married her because of love. But the emotional blockage just would not let the message come through."

The day finally came when Evelyn began to cry in his office. The conversation went like this:

"Evelyn . . . have you asked the Lord to forgive you of this?"

"Oh! I've asked him a hundred times!"

"Well . . . do you believe he has?"

"Oh yes, I believe the Lord has forgiven me—but how can I forgive myself?"

After a pause, the counselor said quietly and slowly, "Oh. Are you holier than God is? If the death of Christ was good enough for God, isn't it good enough for you?"

The woman broke down and wept for ten minutes or more while the Holy Spirit pressed that truth into her heart. Her expression when she finished crying was obviously different. "This is the first time in over twenty years that I feel no condemnation," she said.[8]

While dramatic breakthroughs such as this are certainly possible, in other cases self-forgiveness takes a season of time. People need to hear again and again that forgiveness is real. They need to be around people who reinforce the message, who love them and echo what the Spirit is telling them on the inside. God's love and acceptance becomes genuine as they see it in the faces of God's people.

We can't talk them into it. We can only be like the four friends who picked up the paralyzed man on his mat and carried him to Jesus.[9] When they found the house already packed with listeners, they didn't give up; they got creative and opened a hole in the roof to let the man down in front of the Savior. A great healing took place that day.

That's the key: delivering the needy person to the one who holds all power to change and restore. He gives a new identity, a new capacity to rise and walk with a whole new outlook on life—not because of anything deserved or earned but because of his grace. The truth settles in that "we are God's masterpiece. He has created us anew in Christ Jesus, so we can do the good things he planned for us long ago."[10]

Sometimes the process can be unnecessarily lengthened if the burden of past sin is replaced by the burden of present religion. If the forgiven person is weighed down with new expectations—change the way you dress, change your language, change your hobbies, give up this, that, and the other—they can stagger under a new form of bondage. Paul actually scolded the Galatian believers who were insisting on retaining Jewish rituals when he wrote, "Now that you know God—or rather are known by God—how is it that you are turning back to those weak and miserable forces? Do you wish to be enslaved by them all over again?"[11] He wanted nothing to cloud the freedom that Jesus had died to give them.

This is not to say that lifestyle changes should not occur. But the Holy Spirit is well able to engineer those from within. We don't have to do his convicting work for him.

If self-forgiveness is left incomplete (as had been true in Evelyn's case), it can rise up to haunt a person's steps for decades. Sir Arthur Conan Doyle, author of the Sherlock Holmes mysteries, was a bit of a prankster. He insisted that the most righteous-looking, reputable aristocrat had hidden skeletons in his closet that made him vulnerable to embarrassment. When a group of dinner companions challenged Doyle to prove his theory regarding a certain gentleman, Doyle sent the man a telegram that read, "ALL IS DISCOVERED; FLEE AT ONCE." Sure enough, the frightened man disappeared the next day and was never heard from again.[12]

Open and forgiven hearts, on the other hand, cannot be blackmailed. Those who know, truly know, that God has forgiven their sins—and have forgiven themselves—are free to walk with a clear conscience before the entire watching world.

And God's people need to reinforce this new status. A guy came to our church in Ogden once with a long record of drug abuse and prison time. He embraced new life in Christ with all his heart. He got involved in one of our recovery groups. We were all excited about his spiritual rebirth.

Jay Salas, the recovery group leader, had to be out of town for a couple of weeks, and so he recruited him to set up the room, make sure everything was put away at the end of the night, and lock up the building. But how would he accomplish that?

I (Matt) called him into my office and said, "Hey, let me just give you a key."

This tough guy, with tattoos everywhere and a goatee down to his chest, started choking up. "You'd trust me with that?" he asked, holding on to the key as if it was the most precious thing he'd ever received.

"Yeah, of course," I said.

"Well . . . do you want me to give it back?" he said.

"No, you can hold on to it," I answered. "That way, if Jay ever needs you to do something else for the group, you'll be all set."

His next sentence was this: "I swear to you, man, I'll never break in."

"I know."

"I promise. I'll never steal anything."

"Yeah, I know."

This guy was amazed that someone would actually trust him, given his history. But he was a new creation in Christ. We needed to treat him that way. Never once did I fear that he was going to misuse the key. It was too precious to him, a symbol of his new life.

Sometimes people need very physical, practical evidences of our belief that God has forgiven and redeemed them.

The Hard Work of Forgiving Others

All this progress is at risk, however, if the offender senses reluctance or holding back on the part of the offended. People have a hard time believing God has forgiven them if his people don't.

Granted, it is not easy to forgive the son-in-law who has been beating your daughter every weekend for years. He may now say, "I'm really sorry," but is that quite enough?

It's not easy to forgive the mom who wasted tens of thousands of dollars on drugs, causing her children to lack basic necessities but now says she has repented and will do better in the future.

It's not easy to forgive the husband now sitting in jail, leaving his wife to work two jobs while managing the household alone—even as he claims to have gotten right with God at last.

Perhaps we need to take a deep breath and clarify what forgiveness is and is not.

1. Forgiveness is not just waving your hand and saying, "Ah, no big deal." In many cases, the offense *was* a very big deal, with major ripple effects on multiple people. Reinstatement of trust won't come quickly, if ever.

2. Forgiveness is not making up alibis, as in, "Well, he had a hard life growing up. His parents really didn't raise him very well. He couldn't help himself." There may, indeed, be early influences that were not the best. But they don't excuse subsequent misconduct.

3. Forgiveness is not dependent upon justice being served, as in, "Once they get what's coming to them [from the legal system or whomever], the score will finally be settled, and then I'll forgive." As we all know, sometimes justice never

comes to fulfillment; a crafty lawyer gets the guilty party off the hook, or the bank decides it's easier to write off the debt than to prosecute. Does this trump the need for forgiveness? Not at all.

4. Here is another one: forgiveness cannot be conditional, as in, "Well, as soon as she apologizes, I'll forgive her." You may be waiting a very long time. Some victims we know have gotten up the courage to go confront their parent or other relative about past offenses, only to get surprised with a flat denial: "That never happened. I never did that. You're dreaming up this stuff." Can forgiveness take place even then?

5. Forgiveness is sometimes not quite a one-and-done, in other words, a sweeping statement of pardon that covers all the bases and never has to be reaffirmed. In some cases, it's not quite that simple. For some people, every day brings a new decision to forgive. Offenses of a certain magnitude can only be neutralized over the long haul.

Filling the Gap

So what then is true forgiveness? It is coming to the place of "I love you in spite of all that has happened, and I'm letting it go. I'm not going to keep mulling this over and chewing on it night after night. I choose to release this."

You may think this is humanly impossible. The English language has an adjective: *unforgivable*. Some things do seem so horrendous, so revolting, as to be beyond absolution.

Perhaps they are—until we remember how much God forgave *us*. The Lord's Prayer puts it succinctly: "Forgive us our sins, for we also forgive everyone who sins against us."[13] Jesus went on to elaborate: "For if you forgive other people when they sin against you, your heavenly Father will also forgive you. But if you do not forgive others their sins, your Father will not forgive your sins."[14]

None of us deserved God's forgiveness. None of us could have earned it. All the begging and apologizing in the world would not have sufficed. He had to pay an astronomical price—the death of his Son—to allow for our redemption. Is it not understandable that we should have to struggle to forgive another human being?

C. S. Lewis said it well: "To be a Christian means to forgive the inexcusable, because God has forgiven the inexcusable in you."[15]

It does no good to protest, "Well, actually, I've lived a pretty decent life. Compared to a terrorist or a mass shooter or a ruthless dictator, I mean, come on. My record can't be that bad." In the eyes of the holy God, however, each of us falls short of the mark. There's a disqualifying gap—and Jesus came to bridge that gap. Only through his mercy can any of us be acceptable on heaven's scale.

Having received such amazing grace, it is only reasonable for us to extend that grace to others who have wronged us. In so doing, we present the face of Jesus. Yes, it's costly. But no more costly than what was extended to us.

We can all sit side by side at the King's table because of his undeserved forgiveness and welcome extended to us.

> C. S. Lewis said it well: "To be a Christian means to forgive the inexcusable, because God has forgiven the inexcusable in you."

8

WE HELP RESET
LIVES AND HABITS

When Dallas first showed up at the Genesis Project in Ogden, he wasn't your stereotypical drug abuser. This midtwenties guy was holding a steady job, supporting his girlfriend and their new baby, while continuing to dabble in things that were once much bigger problems. He claimed he wasn't actually *dealing* drugs anymore and had given up meth.

His background, we came to learn, was a mixture of early trouble and glimmers of light. His parents had divorced when he was young. He had grown up from that point with his mom—although he got to spend summers in Wyoming with his dad, a former drug dealer who radically encountered Jesus when Dallas was a teenager. The son was genuinely impressed by the change in his father's life.

His own involvement with drugs, however, kept worsening. As a last-ditch effort, Dallas became desperate enough to enter a recovery program at a rescue mission. While there, he began a real relationship with Jesus, but the Christianity he encountered in the program was extremely hard-core and legalistic. Dallas left the program before graduation and eventually found himself doing a long prison term. But he never quite escaped the memory of his dad's undeniable conversion. He came to us wanting to get his spiritual life in order.

"Hey, I want to meet with you," he said to me (Matt) one Sunday. Revealing his grasp of Christian lingo, he added, "I need somebody to disciple me. I want to figure out how this Christian thing works."

So we began meeting. He was full of questions. "Does God have a purpose or plan for my life? I feel like I'm doing okay right now, but is this where I need to be? What should I be doing?"

I didn't reply, "Okay, I'm going to chart this out for you. First you need to . . . and then next you need to . . . and after that, you need to . . ." Instead, I kept saying, "Let's see what the Lord has to say. Let's open the Bible and get our guidance there." Each week I would give him homework: a passage to read and think about.

He would come back saying things like "Bro, I read that scripture you gave me—and I've got to stop smoking weed, don't I?"

Well, yes, I would answer, that's a fair understanding of what the verses say about our bodies being created by God for wholeness.

"Okay," Dallas would conclude, "I gotta get that out of my life."

The next week, after reading another Bible text, the subject would be different. "Bro, I should probably stop getting drunk, right?" Yep.

Another scripture for another week. Then: "Man, I gotta quit having sex with my girlfriend, don't I?" Yeah.

The week after that: "Bro, I can't stop having sex with her if we're living in the same house. I probably need to move out, huh?" Correct.

Sometimes he would show up angry. "Look, I don't *want* to stop smoking weed! But I have to because that's what Jesus wants from me."

Step by step, Dallas was resetting the true north of his moral compass. I never told him to stop doing drugs or quit having pre-marital sex. He came to these conclusions on his own as we kept focusing on Jesus—who he is, and what he came to do in all our lives.

I cannot report that Dallas evolved into a perfect church boy. He was still Dallas. But he kept engaging with the Word and seeking to do what would please the Lord. He and his girlfriend got married, even though she wasn't thrilled with his change of heart and loyalty.

To this day, a decade later, he will still occasionally come to me hanging his head and mumbling, "Bro, I messed up." This becomes another opening to continue the process of discipleship in a believer who is sincere if not yet flawless. He knows he has veered off course in a bad direction, but the needle is still pointing north in his mind. He wants to get back into alignment.

Who's Driving This Bus?

Scripture says, "Walk by the Spirit, and you will not gratify the desires of the flesh."[1] Another translation puts it this way: "Let the Holy Spirit guide your lives. Then you won't be doing what your sinful nature craves."[2]

This captures the whole of discipleship. The only way forward is not by willpower, not by trying as hard as you can to resist temptation, but by letting the Spirit take over the steering wheel of your life, day by day, decision by decision.

This is much more than sitting through a six-week sermon

> The only way forward is not by willpower, not by trying as hard as you can to resist temptation, but by letting the Spirit take over the steering wheel of your life.

series or an eight-part class. This is a complete upheaval of the old life in order to set up God's new rule in the soul. It is allowing God to inhabit the very center of our lives, learning how to speak, think, act, and feel in sync with who he created us to be. It is replacing the lie of hell that crept into every arena of life with the ever-present promises of God. It is allowing Jesus to sit on the throne of our being.

He will, of course, want to address a number of topics.

Some people—longtime addicts, for example—can't really hear him without first clearing their muddled brains. Before we can start talking about truth, we need to get them detoxed.

Most churches, ours included, are not equipped to provide the twenty-four-hour supervision and medication for the seven to ten days that an alcoholic or opioid addict needs these services. That's a job for the psychiatric unit of a nearby hospital, and it's not fun. Without this level of help, the patient's physical withdrawal may actually turn fatal (unless there's a miraculous intervention of God).

Other substances—methamphetamines, for example—don't require a medical detox. There's no physical withdrawal involved, although the psychological yearnings can be fierce.

In some cases, we meet people whose addiction is so ingrained that they need a longer residential program for a year or so. A number of specialized Christian ministries offer this kind of aid. Their instruction closely matches what we use with nonresidents.

Training Versus Trying

We talk a lot about California pastor John Ortberg's concept of *training* versus *trying*.[3] If you decide to run a marathon tomorrow but haven't been building up your stamina over the past months, you can try as hard as you want. You're still likely to collapse around the second mile. Training, says Ortberg, is arranging your life around the things that will enable you to do what you cannot do now by direct effort.

This is as true in the spiritual realm as it is in long-distance running, mountain trekking, or football. Spiritual disciplines practiced over time give the ability to "keep in step with the Spirit."[4]

Believe it or not, many broken people have tried really hard, again and again, to get their act together. They've failed every time, to the point of giving up hope. To them we say, "Stop trying. Let's train instead. Let's arrange your life around things such as community and worship and prayer and Bible immersion. All of these will help you align yourself with the Holy Spirit. This will be the *direction* of your life, even if it's not the *perfection* of your life."

Randy Crider, whom we introduced back in chapter 3, is famous for pulling together three or four guys for a weekly breakfast. There he teaches them how to arrange their lives around different priorities than they did in the past. He raises very practical questions about how the Spirit wants us all to use our time, to control what we read or watch, to study how we organize our habits and routines. It's actually good training for everyone.

But, of course, this assumes that they're willing to make changes. If not, then we have to step back and talk about core identity. Do we see ourselves as *followers* of Christ or not?

A man came to me (Matt) not long after I had performed his wedding to admit, "Man, I'm struggling with porn. I just can't . . .

it's a noose around my neck. I've had this battle for twenty years, and now my wife found out. It's ruining everything for us."

I replied, "Okay, tell me about your moments of struggle. When are they the most intense?"

"Typically, it's when she's gone. She works days, and I work nights. So it's when I'm alone and bored."

"Where do you get your pornography?" I asked next.

"Online," he answered.

"Okay, let's get practical," I replied. I laid out three possible decisions for moving forward.

"Number one, you can go to the store and buy a simple flip phone—something without a screen or Internet access. It will still let you make phone calls as always, but you'll be removing the availability of all those websites.

"Number two, you can have your wife set up a password on your home desktop that only she knows. You would be saying, 'I don't trust myself to be on the computer when you're not around. So install a password, and don't tell me what it is.'

"Number three, since you talked about boredom, you can make yourself get out of the house whenever you're feeling bored. Go somewhere, change the scenery, put your mind to work on a different topic."

Sadly, the man agreed to the second and third decisions, but not the first. "I can't give up my smartphone," he said. "I'll just try harder."

Too often we are prone to assume we have rights, despite the fact that we claim to have made Jesus the *Lord* of our lives.

Hey, I'm an adult—I have a right to a smartphone.

No, not if Jesus asks that from you.

I have a right to prescription painkillers; my doctor said so.

I have a right to alcohol, in moderation; it's legal, you know.

Folks in Colorado and a few other states now claim the same

thing about marijuana. But if the substance is ruining you, maybe your legal rights have to submit to the higher authority of God, who wants you to live in the wide-open spaces of his freedom. He is always asking us to rise above our emotions and passions, so we can be the people he called us to be.

Years ago, while serving as a youth pastor, I (Rob) was approached by a guy who was a high-functioning alcoholic. He had a great job and had been living with a young woman for the past five years. But now, she had gotten fed up with his drinking and had left. He was devastated.

> Maybe your legal rights have to submit to the higher authority of God, who wants you to live in the wide-open spaces of his freedom.

We began meeting once a week for dinner, just before the church's Wednesday night service, to work our way through the gospel of John. One time I suggested a certain nearby restaurant.

"Man, I just can't go there," he replied. "That's the place where I used to drink a lot. Let's meet somewhere else." And so we did.

Here was a person who knew the exercise of his *right* to drink was not in his best interest as a child of God. He wanted to stay a safe distance from the scene that had trapped him for so long.

Legalism? No. Pragmatism, Yes.

Some might call this legalism. No, it is simply pragmatism—figuring out what is bad for you and getting it out of your life. Another way to say it is this: You can't negotiate your freedom while still in the jail cell. First you must leave the place of bondage, and then you can figure out what to do with your freedom.

Two different times in the epistle of 1 Corinthians, Paul quoted a common saying in his day and rebutted it:

> "I have the right to do anything," you say—but not everything is beneficial. "I have the right to do anything"—but I will not be mastered by anything. (6:12)

> "I have the right to do anything," you say—but not everything is beneficial. "I have the right to do anything"—but not everything is constructive. (10:23)

The spiritual discipline of fasting gives us a good exercise in forgoing something entirely legal and even good (food) in order to achieve something better (the presence of God). It is a way of establishing that *I can actually tell my body no. I am in charge here, not my appetite.*

The same can be applied to any desire that needs to be curbed. This isn't legalism. This is just setting our sights on the greater good.

It's not necessarily easy. But if the motivation is to live life differently from the past, we make changes. We rearrange things. We keep up the training. We say with Paul, "One thing I do: Forgetting what is behind and straining toward what is ahead, I press on toward the goal to win the prize for which God has called me heavenward in Christ Jesus."[5]

The Power of a Group

A great reinforcement of this work is the weekly recovery group, as many churches and other ministries have discovered. It is a safe place where people seeking to reset their moral compasses come together to share how they're doing (for good or not), figure out adjustments they can make, and encourage one another. Some are for men only; some are for women only; others are mixed.

Our philosophy of recovery follows these steps:

1. **Deciding to change and asking for accountability.** This is the starting point. It forces an answer to the question "Am I willing to go into training here?"

2. **Believing in the promise of a better future**—casting a vision of God's better way. The goal is not just to be "okay." It is to dream about becoming whole.

3. **Looking forward to the actual presence of God in one's life**—not only in the emotion of a Sunday morning service but also getting into the Word of God during the week, expecting him to speak, and talking openly and honestly with him through prayer.

4. **Rejecting fear, detours, and shortcuts.** More than once we've heard women say, "I just can't leave this abusive relationship." When asked why not, they reply, "Because I'm afraid. He'll kill me." And the next week they show up at church with another black eye, only to explain, "I fell down the stairs."

    A group leader can press the issue by saying, "Okay, tell us truly why you're afraid."

    "Well . . . I've never lived alone. I've been with this guy since I was fifteen." Or "I just found out I'm pregnant again."

    Chances are, somebody else in the group has been in the same predicament and can tell the story of how she navigated out of it. Somebody else can bring up the fortifying words of Joshua 1:9—"Be strong and courageous. Do not be afraid; do not be discouraged, for the LORD your God will be with you wherever you go." What God did for Joshua and the Israelites facing formidable armies in Canaan, he can do today.

A good road map for groups is the Life Recovery set of materials developed by New Life Ministries.[6] It makes use of the twelve-step outline pioneered by Alcoholics Anonymous—but with a clear focus on Jesus as the only hope for change. The strategy is what Hebrews 12:1–2 says: "Let us throw off everything that hinders and the sin that so easily entangles. And let us run with perseverance the race marked out for us, *fixing our eyes on Jesus*" (emphasis added).

Meetings typically begin with everyone sitting in a circle for a time of worship. Then a leader gives a focal point for the meeting: a Bible passage or a biblical story. "This is what this means to me," he or she will share. Comments and reactions soon begin to flow.

Eventually real-life problems come out into the open. Things like "I had a dope dream last night, and it scared me to death." Or "I woke up this morning with an insatiable desire to go get high." The group leader and other members then show how the power of Jesus can be stronger even in moments like these.

Group leaders, by the way, don't try to cover up their own pasts. Jay Salas in Ogden will openly say things, such as, "Before I came here and found Jesus, my life was a wreck! I was an addicted abuser who was chronically in and out of jail. I had no future, no hope."

Yet this kind of forthrightness has endeared him to many people. He has become an excellent communicator of the Word. He's now full-time on the church staff as our recovery pastor—but if you called him "Pastor Jay," he would shudder at the thought of it.

With all the interaction, recovery group meetings are not short; they can run up to three hours in length. That is because broken people are being listened to, are finding practical steps they can take, and are soaking in encouragement from others just like themselves.

We encourage participants to expand their community, merging seamlessly over time into the larger life of the church. There they continue establishing themselves in God's plan for their lives and relationships.

Lessons Observed

One thing we've noticed in working with people resetting their lives is that serving others is a great antidote to the me-and-all-my-problems syndrome. As we lift their eyes toward helping people in need—for example, our periodic Wanna Give Away outreaches—they grow in spiritual maturity. Even ordinary tasks like setting up chairs or working the check-in counter for children prove valuable.

Related to this is starting to give from what money they have. It may not be a large dollar amount, but it represents rising above personal hoarding to support the work of God. They're starting to think outside themselves.

Not every life will be reset to look exactly like yours or mine, especially if we've had the advantage of growing up in stable, well-organized homes. Not every one of their apartments is going to be spotless. We have to be careful

We have to be careful not to impose middle-class expectations on people who have spent decades in chaos. Instead, we need to let God set the expectations.

not to impose middle-class expectations on people who have spent decades in chaos. Instead, we need to let God set the expectations, "being confident of this, that he who began a good work in [them] will carry it on to completion until the day of Christ Jesus."[7]

Our God takes the long view of all of this, and so must we.

9

WE DEAL WITH ONGOING
COMPLICATIONS

Wouldn't you think that after a troubled man or woman comes to recognize their dysfunctions, receives the grace and forgiveness of God, and goes through the hard work of resetting their moral compass that life should straighten out for them? After all, they've dealt with sin and wholeheartedly set themselves on a new path to follow Jesus. It's all good, right?

Not necessarily.

Certain baggage from the past does not magically evaporate. The person may be *redeemed*, but that does not mean they've been *reinvented*. When Jesus delivered the demonized man in the tombs of Gadara, the fellow no doubt kept carrying the scars on his arms and torso from self-cutting.[1] When the prodigal son was welcomed home again, his father did not offer to split the estate with him a second time; he specifically said to the older brother, "*Everything* I have is yours."[2] There would be no turning back the clock.

The same is often true in today's situations. We have to understand that Jesus' goal is not, somehow, to blow off the ongoing complications in a person's life but, instead, to work around and beyond them, making the individual into the best possible version of themselves going forward. After all, none of us started out with garden-of-Eden innocence. Jesus took every one of us just as we were and lifted us up from that point.

It is not quite fair to say to the new believer, "Just pick yourself up by your bootstraps and make life work! That's what I did." The truth is, many of us were gifted to start with. We won the birth lottery from the beginning. We grew up with stable, loving parents who taught us to be organized, to be disciplined, to apply ourselves in school, to be responsible. Not everybody had these advantages, and the results still show it. Don't try to say your personal gumption and hard work made all the difference.

While some personal behaviors in broken people can definitely be changed by the power of God, other aspects are tough to manage. Here are a few examples.

A Felony Record

Nearly every job application, housing application, or other legal form wants to know if you've gotten crosswise of the law somewhere along the line. The minute this question is answered with a yes, a chill sweeps over the atmosphere. Things get very hard for you. You're instantly disqualified from many possibilities. You've been labeled.

We see this all the time in trying to help people get off the street and rent an apartment. Both of us happen to live and work in cities where affordable housing is tight. An available unit can attract up to twenty applicants almost overnight. If you've had a DUI conviction or done prison time, no matter how long ago, your paperwork will immediately go to the bottom of the stack.

And you've already paid $50 to apply! We've known people who, holding steady jobs, have shelled out $500 in a week trying to rent, and have been turned down ten times.

The city of Ogden, where I (Matt) am based, has an official Good Landlord Program that provides financial incentives *not* to rent to tenants who might "affect the quality of life within our neighborhoods."[3] Davis County, just to the south, has enacted a law that pretty much excludes any violent felon or anyone charged with a sexual crime from living in the county at all. They can't even move back in with Mom and Dad. Many other communities across the nation have similar, if not quite as strict, policies.

While public safety is certainly a valid concern, stop for a moment and consider how this affects the person trying to make a fresh start in life. We cannot estimate how many times we've heard from our people, "I'm trying to do everything right! I'm trying to turn my life around, I'm praying for God to help me—but I'm not getting anywhere."

Employers can hold the same reservations about hiring someone with a checkered history. Why take the risk, they think to themselves, if they've got another candidate who's "clean"? It doesn't seem to matter how much the person wants to work a legitimate job or whether they have dependents to support.

Some people with felonies have said to us, "Look, I know how to survive in the world I left. I know how to make it selling drugs. Maybe I ought to just go back to what I know." They do not resent God; instead, they're frustrated with "the system," as they put it. They feel the deck is stacked against them. "Society" doesn't want them to succeed.

We spend a good deal of time and effort seeking not only to encourage the disheartened but also to make contact with those in the community who might give them a second look.

Personal Appearance

Some people who have lived a tough life simply don't present well. We know one young man who has a tattoo that says "Gangster" right across his forehead! Imagine trying to apply for a job or an apartment with that liability.

We also know a woman, a former dancer at the Fort Collins strip club, who is going to the expense and physical pain of having at least some tattoos removed. She is determined to do whatever she can to erase her social handicaps.

Some people, believe it or not, were never taught how often to take a shower—or that it means more than just letting water run over your body. A little gentle instruction on this (men with men, women with women) can accomplish wonders without making them feel foolish.

If, on the other hand, someone is living out of his car, it can be even tougher to stay clean and presentable. Caring friends are those who don't recoil from the odor or think judgmental thoughts but who, instead, offer viable facilities.

Is this really an issue of discipleship, you ask, instead of just personal preference? We believe discipleship is birthed out of loving relationships, and it is these types of relationships that always encourage the best in every person. Because of this, we believe that discipleship affects every aspect of our lives.

Bad (or No) Credit

The financial lives of broken people are often a disaster. They've borrowed money they haven't repaid. They've ducked out on debts they owe. They've stolen other people's credit cards and abused them.

Some people have never known anything for generations but living hand to mouth. Their parents and grandparents were cash-only people. Everybody just scraped along as best they could, trying to stay alive. If any of us had grown up in that environment, we'd probably be acting the same as they are.

And, of course, the courts are not about to say, "Well, now that you're following Jesus, all is forgiven." This is a complication that has to be dealt with.

We know one fellow and his wife who, back during the era of easy mortgage lending, had somehow managed to buy a house. But they were skipping monthly payments eight and nine months at a time. The bank, knowing the house was in disrepair and couldn't be sold for even close to the balance due, would just renegotiate the mortgage terms, hoping to get back some of their outlay sooner or later.

The guy was oblivious. "This is incredible!" he said. "We get to live in this place without actually paying for it." To him it was a neat way to beat the system—the same system that had cracked down so harshly on him regarding drugs before he came to Jesus. Now it was his turn to get something back.

We had to sit down with him and say, "Okay, wait a minute. Let's not talk about your credit score." (He didn't even know there was such a thing.) "Let's talk about Christian integrity. Let's see what the Bible says about handling debt."

He was amazed: "You mean there's a connection between following Jesus and paying your mortgage? Who would have guessed?"

Keeping a Job

When new believers do manage to get hired despite their records, the next challenge becomes how to fulfill the employers' expectations—like showing up every day on time, putting in a full shift's work, not making dumb mistakes, and so forth. Again, this may be obvious to you and me. But for those who have lived by their wits in the shadows for a long time, it can be a jolt.

We've had to say to guys, "Okay, you've just lost your third job in a row, after only two weeks at each place. What's the common denominator here? Maybe it has something to do with the way you're handling stuff.

"If you continually sleep in . . . if you repeatedly need to stop for gas in the morning instead of taking care of that the night before . . . maybe there's a connection here."

The world of employment is generally quite fair. People don't usually get fired again and again for things that are untrue. What really were the factors that led to dismissal?

A guy came our way in Ogden who had been a drug dealer in New York City but who had been radically saved at Times Square Church. He was forty-four years old, had never had a driver's license (who needs one in NYC?), and had never had a bank account.

He had gone through a school-of-ministry program, similar to a Teen Challenge model, where the day started with several hours of intense prayer, lying on your face before God—which is a good thing. Then came classes on various aspects of the Christian life.

He, of course, had tried to extricate himself from the world of drug selling, which quickly caused him to get shot. He decided to come west and live with his brother. That's how he found the Genesis Project.

We welcomed him and got him a job at a thrift store, which had a Christian manager. It wasn't long before I (Matt) got a call. "We have a problem," the manager told me. "Every time I walk into the break room, this guy is down on the floor weeping and crying out to God. It can go on for an hour! I'm not against prayer, but, hey, I need for him to be working."

I quickly got with the guy to say, "Dude, you can't be praying at work like that."

"Bro, I'm a child of God!" he shot back. "If I feel the need to pray, I just have to—"

"Nope, not at work," I interrupted. "Can't have that going on. You've gotta get your tail out there on the sales floor and do what the boss says. That's why he's paying you."

Such a simple thing. But it was necessary to orient him to diligence in the workplace.

Permanent Labels

Other complications, however, are harder to address. We wrote earlier about felony records. Perhaps the most difficult to overcome is "registered sex offender," which is easily applied and sticks with you like superglue till your dying day. Your name is wide open on public websites for anyone to research with just a few mouse clicks.

Granted, no one wants such a person to re-offend. But the category covers a very wide range, from the monstrous to the incidental. We know a man now forty years old who, in a moment of stupid silliness at age nineteen, dropped his pants and "mooned" a passing school bus. He shouldn't have done that. But now he is stigmatized for life.

Regularly someone in our communities will get on a database

and e-mail us a picture, saying, "Did you know this guy is a sex offender? What's he doing at church, for heaven's sake?"

Our usual response is "Yes, we're aware, and thanks for your concern. We've already talked to his probation officer. Here's our protocol in these cases," and we attach a one-page document. "He will never be anywhere near the children's area. If he needs to use a restroom, he'll be escorted by someone who will go inside first and make sure no kids are around. In fact, he'll have a chaperone at all times."

This is because we have sat down in advance to talk with this person. Our approach has *not* been to say, "We need to protect our children from you." That would drive him right out the door.

Instead, we say, "Let's talk about the fact that people know your past—and that's really hard on you. We are so sorry. We want to make sure that we protect you while you're here at church because just one false accusation against you, and you're sunk. You can't weather that in your life, right?" He readily nods his head.

"So let us make sure you have a safe environment here so you don't have to worry. Let's make sure you're never in a restroom alone with a child. Let's make sure nobody sees you wandering about the children's area and jumps to conclusions that aren't true. We have a specific person who's going to be your friend all along the way; his name is _____. We would hate for you to get into trouble unjustly."

Some registered sex offenders are grateful for this layer of protection. "Yeah, I need somebody to watch my back," they say.

Others, we have to admit, have their pride hurt. "Are you kidding?" they snap. "Do you not understand my circumstances? I've been living under this cloud my whole adult life, and now I have to deal with it even here in church? Just forget it—I'm outta here."

A sad outcome, to be sure.

Restraining Orders

Similar to labeling is when a family relationship goes bad, to the point of one spouse getting a legal restraining order against contact with the other spouse or with their children. Again, these are not hard to acquire in today's legal system.

You may be mortified to think of somebody in your household picking up the phone and calling the cops. But in some families we serve, it's common. Happens all the time.

We deal with these situations regularly, when both husband and wife (or boyfriend and girlfriend) want to keep coming to church. It gets crazy, as we hear ourselves saying, "Okay, Jeff, how about if you come to the early service, just so you're out of the building by ten fifteen, and then Marissa, you can come to the late service."

Then after three weeks go by, you see the two of them sitting together in the same service holding hands! "What's up?" you ask.

"Oh, we're fine," they say. "It was all a big misunderstanding."

The risk is that, if there's a new argument, one or even both of them will end up in jail for breaking the restraining order.

When Sparks Fly

Beyond the occasional spat, it is not uncommon to find couples getting along *worse* after one decides to follow Jesus than they did in their old life. Why is that? you ask. Because in the past they were—to borrow a biblical phrase—"equally yoked"![4] They were united in addiction and chaos.

Now one party has chosen to follow Jesus, and the other party is left saying, "What's up with you? You're no fun anymore! You've turned into some kind of religious fanatic."

The Christ follower winds up in the pastor's office saying, "What can I do? He's upset with me. I want to start tithing, and he says we can't afford that."

Or the man will say, "I'm really getting a lot out of this recovery group—but she says I'm gone too much at the church. She wants us to go out on Friday night and have a good time."

We have to reply that they just keep loving the person they're married to and praying that the life they exemplify will capture his or her heart as well. As Paul writes, "God has called us to live in peace. How do you know, wife, whether you will save your husband? Or, how do you know, husband, whether you will save your wife?"[5] (This assumes that the situation is not physically abusive or adulterous; in those cases, we see scriptural permission to move out, at least temporarily.)

There's an ancillary danger, by the way, when one partner comes to Jesus and the other wants nothing to do with it. Let's say it's the wife who is in church all the time. All around, she's noticing godly men who are exactly what she wishes her husband would be. They love God wholeheartedly. They worship freely. They're spiritual leaders in their homes (she assumes). They're so kind. Oh, if only . . . (What she doesn't want to acknowledge is that the men she's eyeing can be knuckleheads sometimes too.)

If both parties are not careful, this can end up in a tragic affair. We've seen it happen.

Even if both husband and wife have come into a new allegiance to God's way, the adjustments can be jarring. They easily wind up not on the same page. "He says he loves God," a wife moans, "but he doesn't read his Bible as much as I do. I have to talk him into praying with me. I don't know if this is going to work."

Do you want to know something shocking? *It is harder for two broken spouses to get well together than for one person trying alone.* Not just twice as hard. *Ten times* as hard.

How so?

Because each is so enmeshed in the other's habits. They know exactly what triggers what behavior. An example:

A young couple in Ogden came to church and started following the Lord. They weren't married yet, but they really wanted to get clean from drugs. Then he fell off the wagon. She showed up in my (Matt's) office in a panic.

"I'm going to relapse—I just know it!" she cried. "He's bringing it into the house. I can't reason with him. I need help! I need to get out!"

I picked up the phone to see if she could stay a few nights at Ruth House, our home for women in crisis. They didn't have an open bed, but they said they could set up an air mattress. The staff and other women there would surround this frantic girl with love and support.

"Okay, I need to go home and get my stuff," she said. "Thank you so much."

But by late that evening, she hadn't shown up. Nor the next day, or the next, or the next. What happened?

It took more than a month before I saw the couple again. Only then did I learn that she had gone home to pack a bag, saying, "I'm leaving. I'm getting out so I don't mess up again. The church is putting me up."

"Oh, babe, please don't do that," he pleaded. "I really am going to change. I'm going to quit using, I promise. Hey, I have an idea: Let's get high just one more time. I have a little bit of meth left. We can enjoy one last time, and then we'll have the same 'clean date' as we move forward. We'll always be able to celebrate our one-year, two-year, three-year anniversaries together. Won't that be special?"

And that is exactly what happened. Here six weeks later, they both were still high.

There's a reason behind the "equal yoke" metaphor in Scripture. In ancient farming it was actually a safety provision, to keep the stronger ox from hurting the weaker one by stepping on it or jerking sideways. In the same way, God means for a man and a woman to willingly put themselves into a yoke, a formal harness that will keep both parties moving safely in the same direction.

If you're not willing to do that, and you're not already married, then it's time to split.

If they already have children, it's a more complicated story. Somebody has to keep parenting these kids. And somebody—perhaps both adults—needs to keep paying the bills. But this does not mean that the old status quo should go on unchallenged. It's time for the man and the woman to sit down, perhaps with a mature counselor, and wrestle with making a lifetime commitment to each other.

A healthy marriage requires two healthy people. God can bring spiritual and emotional health into any broken life—in which case, we all get to celebrate. But there's no use pretending that unhealthy liaisons will survive long term, let alone thrive. It's not going to happen.

Disaffected Kids

The final complication in our discussion is when kids, especially teenagers, are unimpressed with their parents' dramatic turn to faith. They say things like, "Who are you guys? We've watched you get drunk for years—and now you want us to go to church? Gimme a break!"

It's no fun trying to lead a youth group with kids who don't want to be there.

We've heard some of them say, "When my parents were high, they didn't really care what I did. I could come home at all hours of the night. Now all of a sudden, there are rules? What's up with this?"

Yes, it is possible for the love and kindness of Jesus to shine across this kind of home, so that over a period of time the kids come to want what their parents now have. But it doesn't always happen. Or the game clock runs out; the kids finish growing up and move out on their own. The parents are left with deep regret.

That's how it was when Kim, in his early fifties, began coming to church with his new wife, Gina. He was quiet and unassuming; he had a steady job. Then another man came up to me (Matt) one Sunday and said quietly, "Do you know who that is?"

"No," I answered. "Tell me."

"That's Kim Hughes. He used to be one of the big-time drug producers here in town."

"Really?" I said, surprised. "He seems so gentle now. Sometimes I even see him weeping during the services."

The emotion, I eventually learned by having lunch with him, came from the shame he felt for having alienated just about everyone in his life. He revealed that he had two sons and two daughters from earlier marriages. He admitted he had mistreated them all and he felt awful about it. At this point it would not be an overstatement to say that they all hated him.

Men who have abused their family members can become numb to what they've done—until an encounter with Jesus suddenly snaps them back to the truth. It's almost like ripping a scab off a long-festering sore. Jesus comes along with his saline solution, and it stings! The blood starts running afresh, the green infection starts oozing out, and they're in agony. You tell them that God can cleanse them from whatever they've done in the past, but boy, it's hard in the moment. They literally hate themselves.

On top of this, Kim knew he had hepatitis C from earlier drug needle usage. It was worsening, his liver was failing, and the disease would almost surely take his life. We talked a lot in our get-togethers about eternity, about what lay ahead on the other side. He felt assured that he would go to be with Jesus, but then his thoughts would come back to the present. "Please, can you maybe talk to my kids and see if I could make things right with them?"

I tried. I didn't get far. It got to the point of one son snarling, "What right do you have to give him hope? He doesn't deserve it. And I'm for sure not going to give him hope by forgiving him!"

Never once did Kim blame anyone but himself for this alienation. His heart was too broken.

Death came slowly for this man, after long stretches in the hospital with liver failure. There was no happy ending. God had certainly forgiven Kim, but the grace of God doesn't always erase the consequences.

I conducted his funeral in the church auditorium. I told the large crowd, including some of his old druggie pals, that I was confident Kim had come to know Jesus and was now in heaven. (Pastors are always relieved when they can make this kind of statement; sometimes you honestly don't know what to say.)

Gina wanted to have an open-mic time for sharing. Various people, especially from our church, got up and said things like, "Oh, he was just such a sweet guy. So loving, so gracious."

Finally, one of his sons couldn't take it anymore. He took the microphone and said, "I just need for everybody here to know that the man you're talking about is not the man I knew." And then he dropped the bombshell that turned the audience ice-cold:

"Kim . . . was a devil."

It was significant that he refused to utter the words "my dad." He would call him only "Kim." The young man soon began to get emotional and handed the mic back to me.

Pressing Ahead

When you put your faith in Jesus, he forgives and accepts you, but he doesn't always miraculously fix the damage you've caused. We say to people in these kinds of situations, "You don't have a whole lot of control over what's behind you. But you have so much control in front of you. The promise of Jesus is that, going forward, you can live in freedom with a clean conscience."

We pray with them for a fulfillment of Isaiah 61:3—"a crown of beauty instead of ashes, the oil of joy instead of mourning, and a garment of praise instead of a spirit of despair." God answers those prayers to the extent he can, without stepping on people's individuality. He won't force a resentful daughter to forgive the molestation. He won't force reluctant landlords or parole boards to give second chances. But through all the complications we've discussed in this chapter, the Lord can fortify and lift the spirits of his own to carry on, knowing they have been restored in his sight.

My wife and I (Rob) will never forget the night we were invited to share a meal with a newly redeemed couple. They had originally showed up at a Fourth of July barbecue our church had sponsored, then started coming to services, and gave their lives to Jesus. Both had been addicted to meth. Now they wanted to celebrate their change with us.

When we walked into their lower-level apartment in a rough part of town after the end of our Friday night service, they hadn't even started cooking dinner. But they were so excited to first show us two photo albums. One was of their wedding at the Flamingo in Las Vegas. The other was of their recent baptisms at church! A whole album of pictures.

They proudly pointed out two eight-by-ten frames hanging side by side on the wall: their baptism certificates. "We never used to bother even putting pictures on the wall," the woman said, "because we knew we'd be living someplace only until we got evicted for drugs. This is actually the first place we've ever hung up pictures!" She was jubilant.

And so were we. Regardless of external circumstances and unresolved difficulties, they were experiencing the joy of the Lord's forgiveness. At the core of their living, there could be peace . . . hope . . . and even joy.

10

WE DON'T GIVE UP
WHEN SETBACKS OCCUR

Late-night calls rarely bring good news.

I had gotten to the end of a long day and was just winding down when a familiar voice on my phone blurted out, "Matt—I messed up! My kid [fifteen years old] got mouthy with me, got up in my face . . . and before I knew it, I'd coldcocked him. Can you come over? He's bleeding like crazy."

This father (I'll call him Daren) had made a genuine start to follow Jesus after years of drug abuse. He was giving every effort to develop a Christlike way of living. But now?

I got in my car and headed for his house. There was blood everywhere. Daren fell into my arms, heaving with sobs. Talk about a broken man. The quick-triggered personality he had assumed was dead had suddenly shown up again.

Daren took his son to the ER, where the gash across the teenager's head ended up needing multiple staples to close. The father assumed all this would be his ticket back to prison. But, fortunately, the ER staff didn't ask too many questions.

Before the incident was over, I sat down on the floor and held Daren close. "Man, this is not the end of your story," I said. He was genuinely repentant for his outburst. And, in fact, this turned out to be the last such episode for Daren.

———

I (Rob) was already asleep, and so was my wife, Joy, when her cell phone went off. She managed to fumble for it in the darkness and accept the call.

"Hello?" she mumbled.

"I can't do this anymore!" a woman's tearful voice cried.

It was one of the former dancers at the Hunt Club who had been put out of a job when we bought the place. She had sounded off about that on Facebook and to newspaper reporters in the beginning. But when the seller told her I would love to connect with her and explore ways to help, she and I actually had a great conversation. Joy and I learned more of her story—being sexually abused starting at age four until age twelve, bearing three sons from three different fathers, losing a best friend who was murdered by her husband, who then killed himself. We had helped her with some money for rent and utilities while she went back to work on her bachelor's degree.

"Where are you?" my wife asked on this night. "What's wrong?"

"I'm down in Denver, working a shift at a club," she admitted. "I just . . . my son's birthday is coming up, and I didn't have enough money to buy him a present. So I thought I could . . ." She left the sentence unfinished.

In a few more moments, the facts came out: She had been in the middle of providing a lap dance when suddenly she froze, motionless. The startled customer snapped, "What are you doing? The song's not over!" She threw the man's money back at him and ran for the locker room.

My wife responded in a steady voice, "Here's what to do now: Don't say a word to anyone. Just change clothes, quickly pack up whatever's in your locker, and walk straight out the door. Get in your car and come home. I'll call you again in the morning."

She is doing much better these days, continuing her education while serving as a case worker for developmentally disabled adults. But when your past has been filled with so much treachery, it's not easy to trust even God.

Failure Is Not Fatal

Setbacks in the broken person's walk toward wholeness and a new way of living are not unusual. As much as someone knows in their head that they've been forgiven, life has a way of blindsiding them with unexpected aggravations, and in the blink of an eye they can wind up in the ditch again.

But failure is not fatal. God is still the same loving, restoring God he has always been. He doesn't abide by the three-strikes-and-you're-out rule.

On the human side, setbacks and relapses present something of a double-edged sword. A person's mind can slide in either of two directions:

1. I've blown it, and now there's no hope for me. Nothing has changed. I'm the same old screwup. I'm doomed.

The voice of the Enemy quickly jumps in to say, "That's for sure—you're a lie, a fake. All is lost now. You relapsed! What are you doing going to church? It's time to just leave."

The other direction is an opposite rationalization:

2. Yeah, well, this is fairly normal. Nobody's perfect. Everybody messes up sooner or later. So no big problem. Come on . . . let me just be authentic and real.

In both cases the most vital message for the person to hear is that things can be different this time. God's overall goal is our *transformation*. He loves each of us right where we are—but he loves us too much to let us stay that way. Nothing we do would make him love us more, and nothing we do would make him love us less.

Back to Square One?

A standard premise in the field of addiction counseling is that if a person has been "clean" for a period of time but then relapses, they should not think they're going back to square one—the starting point when they had their first beer or popped their first Ecstasy pill as a teenager. The addict instead picks right up where he or she left off. If he was slamming heroin fourteen times a day, that will be where he resumes.

Guess what? The same dynamic is true on the positive side! If we fall, we don't forget everything God has taught us. We don't have to "get saved all over again." God welcomes us back to the relationship from which we temporarily slipped. Jesus is waiting for us right there, seeking to make us ever more like himself.

Three steps forward and two steps backward is still a step forward. The earlier progress is not forfeited.

Hence, the motto for every believer who has regressed is this: *Fail Fast*. Get it over with already. Learn the lesson, and run to Jesus. Reject the voice of condemnation. Don't dismiss all the hard work you've already invested. You can rise above this.

The apostle Paul, after dealing with a messy situation in the Corinthian church, wrote:

> **Three steps forward and two steps backward is still a step forward. The earlier progress is not forfeited.**

You became sorrowful as God intended . . . Godly sorrow brings repentance that leads to salvation and leaves no regret, but worldly sorrow brings death. See what this godly sorrow has produced in you: what earnestness, what eagerness to clear yourselves, what indignation, what alarm, what longing, what concern, what readiness to see justice done. . . . By all this we are encouraged.[1]

Yes, there truly is a sorrow that leaves no regret. Good outcomes can emerge from bad slipups.

What Family and Friends Can Do

Meanwhile, it is time for those of us who truly care to *move quickly*, proving that we haven't dismissed the fallen person as a lost cause. The individual's inclination to just retreat into a hole and hide must be overwhelmed by the grace and love of moms, dads, brothers, sisters, pastors, lay leaders in the church, and friends on all sides. Time is of the essence here. We must take the step, make that phone call, set up a coffee shop appointment, go see the person who's in jail—reach out any way we can. In this we throw a lifeline to one who's drowning.

This does not mean, however, that we enable destructive patterns to continue. If the person professes allegiance to Jesus, this is not a time for coddling. It does no good to simply commiserate, as in, "Oh, I'm so sorry for what happened to you. Too bad another job fell through" (or whatever).

In fact, the opposite is called for. It's time to say, "You know what? You're more than this. God has a better future for you than this. Stop feeling sorry for yourself, because the truth is, you did this to yourself. You made this choice. Now you have a different choice to make—the better way."

I (Matt) remember visiting a guy who, though having started to follow Jesus, was back in prison for dealing drugs. I said to him, "What in the world! Why are we sitting here again talking through this glass?"

He started to cry as he said, "Man, Christmas was a week away, and I didn't have anything to give my kids. So I just thought this was my quickest path to get five hundred dollars."

Two of Jesus' disciples made major mistakes within hours of each other. The one named Judas "was seized with remorse"[2] and promptly isolated himself, committing suicide. Peter, on the other hand, managed to rise above his denial of Jesus and eventually became a primary spokesman for the faith. Several steps along that path are worth noting.

First, "he went outside and wept bitterly"[3] as soon as he heard the rooster crow. He didn't try to rationalize or minimize what he had done. He owned it—and it made him weep. I (Rob) will sometimes say to the person who has backtracked, "You need to own this—and weep over it. Don't let the prevailing culture tell you, 'Hey, it's okay, nobody should feel guilty about anything.' Let the facts of what you did *break your heart*."

Second, Peter stayed in community with the other disciples—despite the fact that he had just spouted off at the Last Supper about how he would stick by Jesus even if the others didn't. He proved to be perhaps the most blatant failure of them all. Yet by Sunday morning he was in a room with his buddies when Mary Magdalene came bursting through the door to say the tomb was empty. Peter and his friend John jumped up and started running to see for themselves.

Third, he seems to have gotten a special private audience with the risen Lord; at least that is the inference of Paul's summary of cardinal truths in 1 Corinthians 15:3–5, which says "that Christ died for our sins according to the Scriptures, that he was buried, that he was raised on the third day according to the Scriptures, and that *he appeared to Cephas* ["Cephas" is the Aramaic for "Peter"], and then to the Twelve" (emphasis added). You might have thought Peter had disqualified himself from the apostolic group. No, Jesus believed in him more than Peter could believe in himself.

Fourth, he got a new assignment from the Master a few weeks later, after he and six other disciples (again, notice the community support here) had gone fishing all night only to find Jesus waiting for them on the shore as the sun came up. Peter was the first one to scramble out of the boat and head *toward* Jesus, not away from him. They all ate breakfast together, and nobody said a word about what had happened that night around the high priest's courtyard fire. In fact, before the conversation was over that day, Jesus had given him fresh work to do: "Feed my lambs. . . . Take care of my sheep. . . . Feed my sheep."[4]

Jesus gave him a renewed purpose for his life. There was no probation period, no putting him on a short leash until he could prove himself again (which happens all too often in some church circles today). Jesus turned him loose, and by the next month Peter was up preaching to thousands on the Day of Pentecost[5] and working dramatic miracles.[6] Later on, he became the breakthrough Christian emissary to the Gentiles[7] and the author of two New Testament epistles.

Jesus wants to do the same today for those who fall.

The two of us have found that when we give this kind of person a fresh task to pursue, it breaks them out of their puddle of self-centeredness, their obsession with how they messed up, their embarrassment. They begin to serve other people, to participate in something of eternal value. Pretty soon they're saying to themselves, *Wow! God can use me after all. He can push past my failure.*

We have former addicts leading small groups when they're only six months clean. If they hesitate to accept such a role, we say, "Look, there are lots of people watching you who are only six *days* clean. They want to know how you're doing it. How have you made it this far? You know exactly what they're feeling as you look them in the eye. God has a strategic purpose for you and your story."

One Don't, One Do

In all the work of processing a setback or relapse, here are two important words of counsel:

1. **Don't telegraph your disappointment.** Yes, it hurts deeply to see someone go off track after you've invested so much time and love and prayer. But shaming, be it ever so subtle, is not your job. Condemnation is putting yourself up as a wall, a barrier the person has to run through. Are you going to be a barrier or a catalyst?

   Your goal is to keep the focus on restoration. "Man, I'm so proud of you. This time is turning out to be different from all the other attempts in the past, isn't it? Way to go! What else can I do to help you stay strong?" God hasn't given up on this person, and you haven't either. Make sure every communication—verbal and otherwise—carries this theme.

2. **Do let the restored person talk openly about their comeback.** In their minds, they made it up out of the ditch after all! They want to rejoice in how they've recovered. Their testimony may not be squeaky-clean, but it means a great deal to them.

A funny story: At the Genesis Project we set up each baptismal candidate to make a simple three-to-five-minute video that can be shown just before they enter the water. These are always highlights for the congregation, to hear how far the person has come in their walk of faith.

On one occasion at our Provo, Utah, location, a husband and wife were to be baptized on the same Sunday, so we opted to have them do

> Shaming, be it ever so subtle, is not your job. Condemnation is putting yourself up as a wall, a barrier the person has to run through. Are you going to be a barrier or a catalyst?

a joint video. "Yeah, so we've met Jesus," the wife said, "and it's been just so great. I mean, both of us were in and out of prison for years. But since we came to this place two years ago and got into a relationship with Jesus, my husband's been back to prison only twice!"

I (Matt) could just imagine some critic saying, "Good grief, haven't you been discipling this couple?" But then I stopped to remember that in her mind two times in two years was not bad. We opted to let the video run uncut.

At the showing, the congregation chuckled, of course. But then they began to applaud her honesty.

We serve a God who has seen it all, processed it all, and forgiven it all.

We serve a God who has seen it all, processed it all, and forgiven it all. We can take courage from what he said through the prophet Jeremiah after a national skid into sin that resulted in the Babylonian army smashing Jerusalem to bits and hauling most of the population off into captivity:

> "Restrain your voice from weeping
>   and your eyes from tears,
> for your work will be rewarded,"
>   declares the LORD.
> "They will return from the land of the enemy.
> So there is hope for your descendants,"
>   declares the LORD.
> "Your children will return to their own land."[8]

Yes—that's the kind of God we serve today. He never throws in the towel. And neither should we.

WE SHARE THE VICTORIES

The woman in her midtwenties wearing glasses and a blue top looks steadily toward the camera, ready to record her prebaptism video. Her long dark hair is pulled back into a ponytail. Her tone is flat, conveying no more emotion than if you or I said we were going out to get gas or stop at the bank.

But the longer she speaks, the more her composure begins to crack.

My name is Ashley Breidenbach. I'm being baptized today because God cared enough to reach down into my life and save me.

When I was only three weeks old, my mother and I moved here to Colorado to get away from an abusive father. We lived in a safe house for six years. It was during that time that I got trapped in a room by one of the kids and molested.

Shortly after that, my mom and I moved out to a place

in Estes Park [a mountain town, forty miles away]. I remember it was a bit of a happy period. She got me this beautiful porcelain doll. It still brings back good memories; I try to focus on that when I get down.

However, one of my hardest memories is coming home and finding my mom passed out on the couch because she had been using.

When I was nine, my mom decided to clean up her act. She got a job, but she needed a sitter for me. So she posted a sign on the community board in our trailer park, and this man answered the ad. He seemed so nice. He was really awesome. He let me play video games and do things my mom normally wouldn't let me do, like have chocolate.

But he was really anything but nice. He asked me if I wanted to take a walk. When we got to his hotel room, he attacked me—over and over and over again. I remember praying for him to stop, begging him to get off of me. I remember calling out to God, "Please, please, let it stop! It hurts!" But it just kept going on for what seemed like forever.

And then, just before he left, he duct-taped me to the bottom [plumbing] of the sink. He just left me there to bleed out and die.

I don't remember the name of the maid who saved me. I just remember wanting to see my mom, wanting to go home. I remember the pain. And then it got worse. I found out that what he had done to me had caused me not to be able to have children. The doctor said the damage was too severe. I wouldn't be able to carry a child.

After that, my mom relapsed and ended up going to

rehab. She left me with some people she trusted, which in hindsight she shouldn't have. They turned me over to CPS [Child Protective Services] because they didn't want to deal with this broken, messed-up kid. I ended up in foster care.

Throughout my time in foster care, I was in twenty-seven different homes, including group homes. A good majority of them used God as a punishment: You're a sinner, Ashley. You're a horrible person, Ashley. Your mother hates you. God doesn't love you, Ashley. You're going to hell. I heard all these things on a regular basis.

I didn't understand. Nobody had shown me the true meaning of God. Nobody showed me what love was. I didn't know what it meant. I thought I was this horrible, bad person.

I was assaulted and beaten. Starved. One of the foster parents had locks on all the cabinets and the fridge, so if we wanted something to eat, we had to ask. We even had to ask to get a glass of water.

What I mainly remember was hatred and darkness and pure evil.

I tried to commit suicide three times. The rope broke! My foster parents found me in time. I didn't die when I should have.

At fifteen, I started using hard-core drugs. I met a guy who was twenty-nine, and he introduced me to heroin. It made me feel so good. I couldn't feel anything. Not love. Not hate. Not anger. I was numb.

Then I found out I was pregnant—which, to me, was a giant shock. I'd been told I was never going to be able to have kids. And yet I was pregnant. It freaked me out. I went and bought drugs because I was, like, "I can't handle this." In the bathroom, I was getting ready to use. I had everything ready to go. But then . . . I couldn't do it. I flushed the drugs, and it was very amazing to me that I didn't feel any regret at flushing them.

Shortly after that, I got a hot UA [urinary analysis that's positive for drug use]. My parole officer at the time gave me another chance that I honestly didn't deserve. "Ashley, this is it," she said. "Clean up your act now, or you're going to go to prison. Adult prison, Ashley. Not juvie. Not day care. You're going to go to prison, and that's not somewhere you want to be while you're pregnant."

On March 7, 2009, my son was born. He was healthy—and he was mine. For the very first time in my entire life, I knew what it was to love. When the doctor put him in my arms, I cried. "He's so beautiful!" I kept saying.

I decided it was time to change. I didn't want my son to grow up in a world of hate and anger. I had to go back to church.

But when I tried, I felt judged and hated. Here I was, this young single mom with tattoos and piercings and a child who throws tantrums in the middle of church service. I felt like everybody's eyes were on me: "What is she doing here? Can't she control that kid? She should really leave."

Then I came here. I was terrified when my friend Michael suggested that we should come here. I was, like, "I can't do that. I'm not going to take my son to another church where I'll be judged."

But I came. We sat in the very back. I wasn't going to stand up during the songs.

The music started . . . and something happened. I can't explain what I felt. I started crying. Michael had never seen me cry before, and it was very awkward. But it was good. It was a very, very good feeling that I felt here.

I wasn't "Ashley the victim" when I sat in that chair. I wasn't broken. I wasn't nothing. I felt like I was somebody.

And then Pastor Rob started to talk. I remember him saying, "This is the home for the broken."

When we left that day, I told myself I had to come back. I had to feel this feeling again. Where else would I ever feel this?

And my heart started to thaw. It was just amazing. Coming to GP made me realize that I'm not alone. Every time I hid, every time I begged for somebody or something to stop, God was there with me. He never left my side. When I doubted, he was there. When I cursed and hated, he was there. I never realized it. I didn't know what God's love was—that he wasn't just going to give me handouts, but he was going to hold my hand through everything and say, *You're not alone, Ashley. I'm here with you.*

I'm grateful to God for giving me a child when I should have never had one. For giving me a purpose. A reason to wake up in the morning. I see God's love every time I look at my son.

And I'm grateful to everybody who has stuck by my side. Michael. My parole officer. The people I've met here at the Genesis Project. I've never heard a discouraging word since I walked through this door. Ever.

And the fact that they can handle my son in the kids' program is great. Not a lot of people can handle him. But he loves it here, and that makes me so happy. I'm grateful to this church. I really am. I'm grateful to finally feel at home in a place where I never thought I could.

Now it's time to publicly declare my faith in Jesus and be a beacon of hope to other people like me.

By the time Ashley came back up out of the water, there weren't many dry eyes in the place. People clapped and celebrated what God had done in this tragic situation.

A man who worked in our children's ministry and who had been on the receiving end of Ashley's son's outbursts was especially touched. Just the week before, something had triggered the boy, and he began flipping over tables and throwing things. Getting him to calm down had stretched everyone's patience.

At the end of the morning, the man had said to our children's director, "What are we going to do with this kid? Having him here is unsafe for the other kids. Maybe he's just going to have to sit with his mom in the adult service."

The director wasn't sure how to respond. She came to me seeking advice.

"I certainly hear the problem," I said to her. "But if I were you, I think I'd say, 'If that kid can't come to our children's ministry, he can't go anywhere in this city. Where else is he going to go? We exist for him.'"

By the next Sunday, she had not yet gotten around to having that conversation with her staff member. Meanwhile, Ashley's baptism took place. He watched the video and swallowed hard. Going up to our director after the service, he said, "I get it now. I get it. We've got to make this work somehow."

Ripple Effect

Stories such as this are incredibly powerful on many fronts, moving listeners to believe even more strongly in the power of Jesus to rescue desperate lives. It is important to give time and space for their telling. Not just on baptism days. Anytime. In small groups, during Sunday sermons, in coffee shops, even online.

When Jesus delivered the demoniac living in a graveyard, restoring him to sanity and self-control, his parting instruction was "Go home to your own people and tell them how much the Lord has done for you, and how he has had mercy on you." The man did so, "and all the people were amazed."[1]

When Jesus finished talking with the woman at the well who had been married five times, introducing her to "living water" that would change her life, "many of the Samaritans from that town believed in him because of the woman's testimony."[2] They naturally wanted to know what had happened. This woman with the disreputable history, whom they had no doubt shunned up to now, was suddenly the center of conversation. People gathered around on all sides to ask what had happened, who was this remarkable man she had met, and what had he said to her.

In our work at the Genesis Project, we really don't have to run evangelism seminars, trying to coax our people to share their faith. It just happens, through the life stories of victory over darkness. We spend very little on church advertising. Our signage is easy to miss.

The Fort Collins church is on a side street in an industrial part of the city. Meanwhile, the stories do the advertising.

We rarely meet someone after a Sunday service who just decided on their own to come "check us out." Instead, first-timers almost always say, "Yeah, I was talking to Rick [or Melanie, or Larry], and I had to come see what was up."

Sometimes people in need show up because another, more conventional church has recommended us. Word has gotten out that we're a place for addicts, the homeless, and the otherwise broken to find wholeness. That's okay with us; we're not trying to polish an upscale image. We're just trying to seek and save the lost.[3]

The comments are humorous sometimes. I (Matt) got an e-mail not long ago that said, "You won't believe this, but I actually started coming to the Genesis Project because a Mormon bishop told me I would probably fit in better there." Actually, I did believe that. It's a sentiment I've heard more than once while ministering here in Utah.

When God changes a life so thoroughly that it becomes something brand-new, the story travels fast. A broken life restored becomes an occasion of wonder and awe within families and communities. It is like light that travels naturally and quickly. Why? Because that's what light does.

Instructional Value

Our sermons often make way for short interviews or testimonials right in the middle of a point. When I (Rob) preached on disappointment with God, I brought onstage a couple who had lost a baby. Their telling of what happened, how much it hurt, and how

God carried them through that tragedy was more powerful than any description I could have uttered.

If the subject is mental purity, I might bring up a construction worker who will sit on a stool and talk about his ten-year battle with porn. As he speaks, every guy in the room who is struggling in this area will be listening intently, wanting to hear how he gained victory. They will find

> When God changes a life so thoroughly that it becomes something brand-new, the story travels fast.

hope that if this guy cleaned up his fantasy life, they can do the same. It's a lot more effective than any sermon I could preach.

And whatever the topic, I notice that after the service, people will cluster around the interviewee, wanting to know more. They're drawn to connect with someone who has overcome the same traps they are battling, whether it's drugs, parenting problems, porn, or anything else. They end up making appointments to have coffee together.

The story has to include both the failure (the wages of sin) and the victory. It is not told for shock value. Its purpose is redemptive, educational, enlightening. It must end up showing what God can do in a messed-up life.

More Ripples

Even outside the church, stories of change have a way of making fresh connections. Ashley Breidenbach and her son had nothing in common with a much older man named Gary, who lived in the apartment next to them. But they became close friends. After Gary had a near-death experience in which Ashley called 911 and performed CPR to save his life, she felt compelled to invite him to church. He accepted.

The first time I (Rob) saw him, I thought by his disheveled look that he might be homeless. Ashley clarified that for me. And the next Sunday, he was back. He became a regular.

Then one Sunday in April 2017, Gary got up the courage to say to me, "Um . . . I was just wondering . . . how do you know if you're ready to be baptized?"

I sat down with him immediately and unpacked what it means to trust Jesus with your life. I talked about responding to his love, grace, and forgiveness.

"I think I've done that," he replied. "I think I need to be baptized now."

I happily explained the process of meeting with a certain volunteer to outline what he would say in his video, and then setting a time to record the clip.

"Well, I really don't like to talk in front of people," he said. "Actually, I was wondering if I could get baptized next Sunday. It will be my sixtieth birthday. I would really like that."

"Okay," I said. "The video isn't mandatory. Maybe we'll just have Ashley stand up ahead of time and summarize your story. Then you can be baptized!"

That is what happened. It was a joyous occasion.

Less than a month later, Ashley stopped by one evening to check on Gary. She knocked on his door. No answer. She banged more vigorously. "Gary! Are you in there? It's Ashley."

No response.

Now worried, she went to see the property manager, who came with a master key. They opened the door—and there was Gary, dead in his chair from a heart attack.

He had given his life to Christ just in time.

The next time I talked with her, I said, "Ashley, do you realize that God used you in Gary's life? Think about what has happened over the last nine months. It's incredible!"

This whole experience has made her even more passionate about sharing God's love with people in need. Through her job at Catholic Charities (where she is doing very well and recently got a promotion), she has developed a huge concern for the homeless.

Once a month on Wednesday nights, we have a different kind of service that is just worship, prayer, and Communion. I sometimes focus on a theme for the night, asking various people to lead segments of prayer. On the night I zeroed in on homelessness, I asked Ashley to lead us.

She stood up and began praying with boldness, then weeping as she pleaded with God for people in our city whom no one cared about. Soon everybody in the room was bawling. It was a powerful season of intercession.

One breakthrough in one person's life leads to another, and another, and still another. The weak become strong, and soon they lift others up from the shame and darkness that has engulfed them for so long. One story of victory turns into two, then three, then even more.

In so doing the light of God's love becomes multiplied.

12

IT'S SIMPLE
(BUT NOT EASY)

Helping to redeem the life of a person beset by dysfunctions and bad consequences may sound daunting. But, in fact, it isn't as complex as you might assume. The secret lies not in programs and systems and behavioral theories. It is rather a matter of *getting people to the feet of Jesus.*

We say this based on our dogged belief that he can do what we humans, however well-meaning, cannot. It's the difference between natural approaches and the supernatural. Broken people have, in fact, already tried a lot of human systems. They've gone to rehab. They've gritted their teeth and made resolutions. They've heard speeches from their parents, their friends, their probation officers, from judges, from society at large. They've been told to get their act together. What they haven't yet experienced is an encounter with Jesus.

Yes, they bring obstacles to the process—bad memories of family when they were younger, low self-esteem, lack of self-discipline, bad memories of church, legal constraints following criminal activity—the list goes on and on. But Jesus is the Greater One. He has never been stymied by our barriers, and neither should his people who have a heart to care.

Repeatedly in the Gospels, we see people humbly bringing their desperate acquaintances to the Master's attention:

- The royal official with the critically ill son[1]
- The Roman (non-Jewish) centurion whose servant was about to die[2]
- The father of the convulsion-plagued boy, who didn't give up when the disciples proved powerless to help[3]
- The four friends who carried the paralyzed man toward the house where Jesus was speaking, and would not be deterred by the standing-room-only crowd[4]

That's all they knew to do. And they trusted Jesus to go to work on impossible situations.

No Formula

Making this kind of connection can require persistence. Relationships often take time—lots of it—to get to the point where the broken person is willing to trust us in our claim about Jesus' power. It may not happen in one conversation or one church service.

But this must not divert us into thinking we need to come up with a better strategy. Jesus was not kidding when he told his disciples at the Last Supper, "Apart from me you can do nothing."[5] Hadn't he already poured three years of training into them? Weren't they pretty smart about ministry by this point? Apparently not enough to make a difference in the big world they were about to enter.

The same is true today. If there were a formula for permanently changing messed-up people, somebody would have written a book about it long ago and made a fortune. Sermons by themselves don't do the trick (we preachers tend to forget this sometimes). We don't change people with three creative points and a nice conclusion. Motivational speeches wear off within an hour or two.

In fact, that may be why so many people in our culture have become "de-churched." Once upon a time, perhaps in their youth, they went to church and heard a lot of polished oratory. But it didn't stick. Their lives kept spiraling from one mess to another. Now they never darken a church door except for somebody's wedding or funeral.

Jesus is the one who does the changing. Dick Foth, whom we mentioned back in chapter 6, has a saying: "Jesus plus nothing changes everything." He holds up a glass of water and asks the audience, "What is this? We're supposed to drink eight of these a day, right? So what is it?

> **If there were a formula for permanently changing messed-up people, somebody would have written a book about it long ago and made a fortune.**

"You all know the answer: two parts hydrogen, one part oxygen. Very simple. If you go without this about four days, you're going to die.

"Meanwhile, you wash your car with this liquid. You water your lawn with it."

Then he holds up a can of Coke. "Guess what," Dick continues. "This is mostly water—with a few additives.

"But you'd never wash your car with Coke. You'd never water your flowers with it. The additives haven't made it better at all."

His point: *When we add stuff to Jesus, we dilute him at best—and at worst we make him toxic.* If we will just let him be who he is, full strength, he will sustain and purify our very lives.

The words of Simon Peter echo throughout time, uttered when Jesus asked the twelve disciples if they wanted to leave him and go try a different approach: "Lord, to whom shall we go? You have the words of eternal life."[6] It almost sounds as if Peter was admitting, *I sure don't have any better ideas. You're the one and only source for everything we need.*

Ground-Level Help

Weekend services have a place in conveying this message, but they are definitely not the center point. They can cast a dream of what could be. Far more important is for an individual believer to connect and bring hope, one person at a time. Time and again the two of us have seen a concerned relative or friend reach out to the broken person and get further, faster than we can.

Brandon and Mandy Kay have become good examples of this. Things certainly didn't start out on a good footing, though. A few years ago, Mandy started coming to our Ogden church by herself. I (Matt) still remember the day she came into my office for an appointment. Her basic message was "I'm separated from my husband. We're getting a divorce. I've got a boyfriend now." She seemed to want my approval for this course of action.

We talked about what God's plan is for marriage. She listened.

Soon after, I got to meet Brandon. To make a long story shorter, God reconciled their marriage. Mandy got rid of the boyfriend, and the couple pursued a joint walk with Jesus. In fact, Brandon got involved in the work of a halfway house, to which we sent a bus each Sunday for residents to be able to come to church. He fell in love with this outreach.

Then one Sunday, who should step off the bus but the former boyfriend. The guy Mandy had lived with for a year. In fact, the guy who had treated her terribly.

Brandon came to me saying, "Man, I'm struggling with this. Just seeing him made my stomach roll over."

"Yes, I get it," I replied. "That's got to be tough for you. What do you think God wants in this kind of sticky situation?"

He wasn't sure. But a week later, he came back to me. "I've really prayed about this," he said. "I think God has called me to disciple this man . . . just walk with him toward Jesus."

And that is what has happened. It all started to blossom when Brandon went up to him and said, "I care about you. And I forgive you, because I don't know what else to do." From that day forward, Brandon (with his wife's full blessing) became a spiritual father to this man. I look out from the platform on Sunday mornings and see all three of them in the same service.

Simple. Certainly not easy, but simple.

Brandon, in fact, was the one who picked him up from jail to go reclaim his driver's license after a DUI charge. He's helping the guy put the pieces of his life back together. He's guiding him to reset habits and patterns under the lordship of Jesus. Meanwhile, Mandy is cheering her husband on in this vital ministry.

If that guy had remained just a face in the crowd on the thirteenth row, he would likely have been overlooked. I doubt I would have been able to reach him. But Brandon could and did. This was the "community of the imperfect" at work—those who have been redeemed from the pits of sin and self-destruction now showing others the path to Jesus.

The apostle Paul put it this way:

> Brothers and sisters, think of what you were when you were called. Not many of you were wise by human standards; not many were influential; not many were of noble birth. But God chose the foolish things of the world to shame the wise; God chose the weak things of the world to shame the strong. God chose the lowly things of this world and the despised things—and the things that are not—to nullify the things that are, so that no one may boast before him.[7]

Simplicity Is Not Shallowness

However, no one should think that keeping the gospel simple means giving up substance. Jesus' offer of change is a straightforward message—but it puts every man or woman on the spot to make a response. There is a big difference for us all between stating our doctrinal beliefs and actually trusting God enough to obey him when it's hard. We can quote Scripture and expound on finer points of theology without facing the question of lordship. Will we surrender to him, or will we continue to be our own king?

Whatever the struggle is in a person's life, whether addiction or sexual deviance or violent temper—or pride or materialism or jealousy— the issue is who's going to be on the throne.

That was certainly true of the rich

> Jesus' offer of change is a straightforward message—but it puts every man or woman on the spot to make a response.

young ruler who came to ask Jesus what he had to do to inherit eternal life. Jesus started out by walking him down somewhat of a rabbit trail—had he obeyed this law, that law, the other law? Things were getting complicated as the man proclaimed his virtues.

But then, Jesus cut to the chase: "You still lack one thing" (notice: not two, not five, not twelve). "Sell everything you have and give to the poor, and you will have treasure in heaven. Then come, follow me."[8]

And the man walked away because he felt what Jesus asked of him was too hard.

It is folly for us to present a relationship with Jesus that costs little. When we start sentences with "*Just accept him* as your Savior" or "*All you have to do* is pray this *little* prayer," we are telegraphing that we think salvation is not that hard a deal. We are selling short the epic life change Jesus had in mind when he said, "Whoever wants to be my disciple must deny themselves and take up their cross daily and follow me."[9] And when he used the metaphor *cross*, he wasn't talking about a nice piece of jewelry around our necks. He was talking about an instrument of death.

The curious thing is, messed-up people are often more willing to say yes to the tough call than rich young rulers. They already know what death feels like. They've been living in havoc for years now. They're desperate enough to respond to the sober option of making Jesus their king at last.

Other people tend to equivocate, to rationalize, to try to bargain or finesse the matter. They are a bit like Peter in his early days with Jesus. After Jesus used Peter's fishing boat as a platform for teaching a crowd of people, he gave him an instruction: "Put out into deep water, and let down the nets for a catch."

Peter respectfully tried to explain that this probably wasn't going to work. After all, he was a professional fisherman. He knew the waters of Galilee well. He knew what times of day to cast out the nets, and when not to bother. He'd already been pursuing his trade throughout the night.

But then Peter added the four words that would change his life: "But *because you say so*, I will let down the nets."[10] The result was dramatic that day (a huge catch of fish) and for the rest of Peter's life. He locked in on a lifestyle of "because Jesus says so."

Simple.

The Bible includes another story that didn't work out so well. It is Eve's conversation in the garden of Eden with the serpent. God had clearly said something: "You must not eat from the tree of the knowledge of good and evil."[11]

But well, now, did he really mean that? The serpent wanted to know. Maybe Eve and her husband had misunderstood. Or maybe God was holding out on them, keeping them from something good. The discussing and negotiating got into full swing, until the couple ended up slip-sliding away from the divine mandate. The result turned out to be tragic.

The clear-cut, straightforward call of Jesus is the only route to wholeness. The two of us have learned over the years that when we sit with a troubled person, we need to say, "I am not your answer. I can't fix you. I can't patch up what's broken in you. But Jesus can. Do you want to turn loose control of your life with all of its issues and let him do that?"

Temptations to Overcomplicate

Granted, this goes against the grain of our culture's practicality and tendency to hunt for our own solutions to problems. We Americans are intrinsically pragmatic people, always looking for the next theory or scheme that will solve current problems. We get impatient. We want some new approach that will produce results by next month.

For example, what about behavior modification? It is said that if we could adjust the way people think, it would change the way they act, which, over time, would change their core being. This assumes, of course, that people really can drum up the power to change from within.

While certainly there are insights in the study of psychology that shed light on why people behave in the ways they do, the missing element is the outside power to redeem. The moment we start building human systems and programs, we divert ourselves from what Jesus alone can do. Believe me, the two of us have made this mistake more than once. We've come up with some fairly complicated strategies over the years—and every time, we seem to end up the worse for it. We've looked for easy answers and shortcuts, and they never turn out quite right. We find ourselves disappointed.

We've had to relearn the wisdom of the old acronym KISS (Keep It Simple, Stupid!), which is attributed to a Lockheed aeronautics engineer back in the 1960s best known for his work on designing the U-2 and SR-71 supersonic reconnaissance jets. He is said to have given his team a handful of tools, and the mandate to design parts that an average mechanic could repair in the field under combat conditions with only those specific tools.

> The moment we start building human systems and programs, we divert ourselves from what Jesus alone can do.

The same principle applies, we have learned, to the mechanics of congregational life. At the Genesis Project we don't deploy people to numerous boards and committees, for example. Church politics are virtually unknown. Yes, we admit that logistical hiccups and glitches occur from time to time. But our main goal is to move believers—including ourselves—toward the hard work of building one-to-one relationships with broken people for the purpose of introducing them to Jesus. He is the only one who can repair the damage of sin.

PART THREE

BEAUTY
IN THE
BROKENNESS

THE ART OF
SPIRITUAL *KINTSUGI*

If you've ever dropped a piece of cherished porcelain or other ceramic onto a hardwood floor—an exquisite vase, your child's kindergarten masterpiece, your great-grandmother's special teapot—you know the feeling as you stare at the broken pieces. *Oh no! Now it's ruined!*

Maybe not.

Japanese artisans for several centuries have perfected a craft called *kintsugi* ("golden joinery"), in which they take the fragments and put them back together again—trying not to conceal the cracks but rather to highlight them. They use a special lacquer mixed (or sprinkled) with gold, silver, or platinum, accentuating the jagged lines. (To see dramatic pictures, do an online search for "*kintsugi*.") The result is an intriguing work of art that tells a story and can even command high prices in the fine-arts market. Gifted pottery artists in multiple places—Taos, New Mexico, for one—have made this their specialty. Exhibits regularly show up not only in Japanese museums but also in such prestigious venues as New York City's Metropolitan Museum of Art and Washington's Freer Gallery at the Smithsonian.[1]

The Japanese say this is an outgrowth of their philosophy of *wabi-sabi*, a belief in the beauty of imperfections. What an excellent metaphor to illustrate God's intention for broken lives. Men and women who have fallen and cracked themselves into a dozen or more fragments can be redeemed. They may not look the same as they could have looked. But instead, they can take on a new, even exquisite beauty. Maybe this is part of what Ephesians 2:10 is talking about when it says, "We are God's handiwork, created in Christ Jesus to do good works."

Unique

No two *kintsugi* pieces are alike. Each has its own character and style. So it is with lives restored. Some people's "cracks" are, in fact, beautiful.

Before I (Rob) came to the Genesis Project, I pastored a congregation that included evangelist Nicky Cruz and his family. Millions have read his story in the bestseller *Run Baby Run*—how God rescued this violent, out-of-control gang member on the streets of New York through the ministry of David Wilkerson (who went on to found Teen Challenge). I always loved to have Nicky speak in our church whenever he wasn't out holding a big crusade somewhere around the world.

Nicky's first language is Spanish. His English still isn't all that smooth. He talks fast, and you have to concentrate to get what he's saying, guessing at some of his pronunciations. But it doesn't hinder him one bit! When he calls audiences to surrender to Jesus, teen-agers and adults rush to the front. He is a mighty tool in the hand of the Lord.

Thank God nobody told Nicky Cruz he needed to be another David Wilkerson or anyone else. His "broken" English is a beautiful thing.

God takes each of us the way we are, patches our unique frag-ments together, and puts us to use for his purposes. He is the master craftsman.

What's the Backstory?

Nearly every time someone looks at a piece of *kintsugi* pottery, they can't help asking, "So what's the story here? It's beautiful! But how did this come about?"

The owner doesn't take very long telling how the piece origi-nally got broken. Maybe a sentence or two, but quickly they're on to how the restoration work was done, who the potter was, what mate-rials were used, and how the person managed to buy the finished product in the end.

The main point in any broken and restored person's testimony is not how bad they used to be. That is only a prelude to highlight-ing what Jesus has made them to be today. This inspires hope in the listeners, who may have tried to hide their own cracks for decades. Now they start to think that maybe God could fill those cracks with gold as well.

Many guys at the Genesis Project volunteer to go back into the jails and prisons where they were once incarcerated and tell their stories. If they sit down with an inmate who says, "But you don't know about . . . ," they can quickly say, "Oh yes, I do. I used to live right over there in cell 28B. Wanna know how my life got radically changed?"

Jay Salas, whom we introduced at the beginning of chapter 3, was speaking in one prison when a guard eyed him closely. At the end of the meeting, the guard motioned him into a back room to talk. Jay started to freak out. What was going to happen?

"What's your name?" the guard barked.

"Jay."

"What's your last name?"

"Salas."

"No, that's not right," the guard declared.

"Well," Jay explained, "my legal name is still Jay England. But my stepfather who raised me was Salas, so that's the name I've always used." On his birth certificate, Social Security card, and every arrest warrant, however, the surname was England.

"England—yup, that's right," the guard said. "Do you know what? I'm the cop who arrested you back when you were a teenager and shot that kid!" He went on to explain that he had planned to make Jay his first RICO (racketeering) case, in light of Jay's membership in an organized gang. This would have been a boost to the cop's career.

"Man, I spent a lot of time hating you and the guys you ran around with," the guard continued. "And when they didn't charge you as an adult, and you got the ability to 'walk,' it really ticked me off."

Jay's hands grew clammy at this moment, wondering what would happen next.

But then the guard became soft as he uttered his next words: "It all makes sense now . . . it all makes sense now." Were those actual tears in his eyes? Jay couldn't quite tell.

"Keep coming in here," the guard said as he turned to leave. "These guys need you."

Spiritual *kintsugi* on display.

Oak Trees

This is what the prophet meant when he predicted that Christ, the Anointed One, would "give them beauty for ashes."[2] And more than just fragile beauty; the same verse goes on to say, "They will be called oaks of righteousness, a planting of the LORD for the display of his splendor."[3]

An oak is a *strong* tree. It's no pine or spruce or redwood that can be blown down or snapped in a windstorm. An oak is sturdy, deeply rooted, durable. Human beings whom God redeems and restores have the capacity to keep displaying God's splendor year after year, through easy times and hard times. Nothing quite shows God's power like a life that has been raised out of the depths of darkness into the beautiful sunshine of his glory.

14

THE GOSPEL STILL
WORKS—HERE AND NOW

Do you believe that the gospel still works today? Truly? If you are a churchgoer, of course you're going to say yes. But down deep inside, are you sure about that?

For more than a few Christians, there's a tinge of unspoken doubt: *Is this salvation thing maybe a bit of a sales pitch?* they quietly wonder. *Just a come-on to get people in the door? It sounds good, and likely works for most regular people, but not hard-core sinners or people with mega-problems that seem unsolvable and unforgivable.*

That is not how the early apostles felt. They believed 100 percent that the gospel was a game changer. They claimed it had the power to revolutionize the messy Roman culture with all its violence, injustice, dysfunction, and personal pain. They were willing to get beat up, jailed, and even martyred for this belief.

How were they so sure? Because the gospel had changed *them* personally. Paul wrote that he was *eager* to get to the massive, intimidating capital of Rome to preach the gospel.[1] It didn't scare him at all.

Imagine that you're an evangelist in present-day America or Canada. Where would you prefer to hold public meetings? The Bible Belt? Midwestern farm country? Conservative suburbs? Paul had preached in a lot of ordinary places across the empire, but now he was saying he couldn't wait to tackle Washington. New York City. Toronto. The toughest, most sophisticated, most skeptical crowds would be fair game for the hope of the gospel. After all, it had broken through the hard crust of *him*.

To his apprentice Timothy he boldly wrote:

> Even though I was once a blasphemer and a persecutor and a violent man, I was shown mercy because I acted in ignorance and unbelief. The grace of our Lord was poured out on me abundantly, along with the faith and love that are in Christ Jesus.
>
> Here is a trustworthy saying that deserves full acceptance: *Christ Jesus came into the world to save sinners—of whom I am the worst.* But for that very reason I was shown mercy so that in me, the worst of sinners, Christ Jesus might display his immense patience as an example for those who would believe in him and receive eternal life.[2]

"The worst of sinners"—a blunt admission. If you think you've done Jesus a favor by coming to him and attending church, you won't be using that kind of terminology. But the truth is, Jesus has rescued each of us from the same pit as the addict, the wife beater, the extortionist. None of us could have scratched and clawed our way up out of the pit of sin on our own. The whole notion that we could put ourselves back together is fundamentally untrue. It's anti-grace.

Jesus did not come to take pretty decent folks and make them a little more middle-class.

Week after week, I (Rob) watch a certain man weep through our service who is a registered sex offender for molesting a child. He's probably sixty years old now.

Recently he came up to me at the end of the morning. "Would you just bless my new Bible?" he timidly asked, holding out the cheap little paperback NIV Bible we'd given him. I said of course I would. I prayed that God would open the words of this book to give light and understanding to this dear man, who is being transformed by the gospel.

Of course, he's going to have to carry the baggage of what he did for the rest of his life. Even among criminals in prison, there's nobody more despised than a guy who molested a child. Here on the outside, society will make it tough for him. In church, we're not ever going to let him hang out in our children's area.

> Jesus did not come to take pretty decent folks and make them a little more middle-class.

But Jesus is renovating him from top to bottom. He is teaching this man how to think differently, how to avoid the triggers that would get him back into trouble, how to accept that he is, indeed, a son of God and headed for heaven. You and I are going to be his neighbors up there.

Filling the Vacuum

Blaise Pascal, the brilliant French mathematician and inventor in the 1600s, is often quoted by Christians as saying, "There is a

God-shaped hole in every human being that nothing else can fill," or words to that effect. Historians have not yet been able to find that precise wording. But what Pascal did say in his masterpiece *Pensées* is a more developed version of the same thought:

> What else does this craving, and this helplessness, proclaim but that there was once in man a true happiness, of which all that now remains is the empty print and trace? This he tries in vain to fill with everything around him, seeking in things that are not there the help he cannot find in those that are, though none can help, since this infinite abyss can be filled only with an infinite and immutable object; in other words by God himself.[3]

For all our modern intellect, our contemporary innovation, our impressive technology, our self-help TV shows and websites, our growing psychological understandings . . . can we claim that humanity is getting better? Healthier? More centered and peaceful within the soul? Not really. It seems people today are more bound, more broken, than ever. We need help from above. We cannot be good enough without God.

Paul, though well educated, admitted as much when he wrote to the Corinthians, "Where is the wise person? Where is the teacher of the law? Where is the philosopher of this age? Has not God made foolish the wisdom of the world? For since in the wisdom of God the world through its wisdom did not know him, God was pleased through the foolishness of what was preached to save those who believe."[4]

He said much the same to his readers in Thessalonica, where he had lasted less than a month[5] before being driven out of town. Yet a solid community of believers was established. How?

Our gospel came to you not simply with words but also with power, with the Holy Spirit and deep conviction. You know how we lived among you for your sake. You became imitators of us and of the Lord, for you welcomed the message in the midst of severe suffering with the joy given by the Holy Spirit. And so you became a model to all the believers in Macedonia and Achaia.[6]

All his education at some of the best schools of his time was not enough to change lives. Only the gospel combined with powerful demonstration could accomplish that.

If any of us thinks that "Jesus saves" sounds like a cheesy Christian cliché, it must not deter us from the truth it embodies. Jesus really does rescue the broken, the messed-up, the disturbed, the restless, the addicted, and all the rest of us sinners. He transforms us into something we never thought we could be. Jesus really can turn us around.

And he can do it *now*, in the present. Not just back in Paul's day or any previous era. Nor only in the future, at the end of time. *Today.* The story of Mary and Martha, the distraught sisters who had just lost their brother, Lazarus, is instructive here. When Jesus finally showed up in their village, Martha complained, "Lord, if you had been here, my brother would not have died." Mary said the same thing a few minutes later. They both felt Jesus could have been effective *in the past*, a few days earlier, when Lazarus was still breathing.

Jesus responded to Martha, saying that, in fact, "Your brother will rise again."

Now she switched to focus on the distant future. "I know he will rise again in the resurrection at the last day."

That wasn't what Jesus had in mind, either. He proceeded to bring life to the already-buried body *that very day*.[7] His power could not be compartmentalized to either the historical past or the eschatological future.

Go Ahead and Say It

We must not be afraid to verbalize this to our friend, family member, work colleague, neighbor, or other person in need—*if we have the relationship in place to do so*. In a context of genuine love and care, the gospel can be received as the very good news that it is.

> If any of us thinks that "Jesus saves" sounds like a cheesy Christian cliché, it must not deter us from the truth it embodies. Jesus really does rescue the broken.

Without the relationship, however, the words will come out trite, sterile, even offensive. That is why this book has spent so much time emphasizing the importance of hearing people's stories and walking alongside them through their turmoil.

But we must be convinced ourselves that we're speaking the truth about redemption. We must believe that evil and God are not equal foes. When Jesus called us to kick down the gates of hell,[8] he didn't for one minute see it as a fair fight. Darkness never stands a chance against light. He is the Light of the World.

People say to the two of us, "Oh, you can't go into such-and-such a neighborhood at night." Sure we can—not to be reckless but to trust in the protection of the Overcomer. This doesn't mean our buildings haven't been vandalized occasionally. Still, we keep turning up the Light. It must not be squelched.

C. T. Studd was a national cricket star in England, from a well-to-do family. At age twenty-five, he left the world of sport to spend the rest of his life taking the gospel first to China, then to southern India, and finally to central Africa, where he died in 1931. His attitude shines bright in this verse he wrote:

> Some wish to live within the sound
> Of Church or Chapel bell,
> I want to run a Rescue Shop
> Within a yard of hell.[9]

He, like the apostle Paul and many others, ran *toward* the battle instead of trying to huddle in a safe alcove. He refused to be intimidated. He fully embraced the bold call of Christ to *come and die*. Too many Christians today are more interested in "come and chill." They want a religion that costs as little as possible—Jesus as a hood ornament.

Following the real Jesus may turn out to be costly, and we do no one a favor to hide that fact. But the benefits far outweigh the price.

Last Words

The power of the gospel was seldom displayed more poignantly than in the baptism video we at the Genesis Project–Ogden prepared with Larry Kautzman, a sixty-something man riddled with cancer who had recently come to Jesus. In a shaky voice he sat in a chair and told how he had dropped out of a traditional church at age thirteen, never going back until recently. He now began tracking the progression:

"In January there was no Jesus—just a can of Bud Light, a few cuss words, and a pool game to win.

"In April I was devastated when the doctor said, 'You have three months to live. If I pull out all the stops, you might get up to eighteen months.'

"By October I was still alive, but things had really fallen apart medically. I started looking for the Lord. I started to see what religious folks had always seen."

Larry and his wife, Shelley, began growing in their walk with Christ even as his disease worsened. Over the next year they learned how to pray. They began telling anyone and everyone about Jesus.

"Now I'm being baptized," he continued in the video. "It's the Lord and me for the rest of my life. I'm not gonna let him go."

Looking straight into the camera, he continued, "I don't want to die. But I'll probably die before any of you guys do. I'm going to a better place. I'm a true believer now." And with that, he broke into a big smile.

We shot this video on a Wednesday, intending to use it the following Sunday. But on Friday, Larry's health took a sudden downturn, and he reentered the hospital. None of the prognoses were encouraging. So we took the unusual step of baptizing him by aspersion (sprinkling) there in his hospital room on Sunday afternoon.

He died about four hours later.

No web is too tangled, no life too trashed to be redeemed by the gospel of Jesus.

We ended up showing the video at his funeral. I (Matt) stood up afterward and said, "What a privilege that we just got to witness Larry preaching the gospel at his own funeral. I don't really need to say much more, do I?" It was an awesome, never-to-be-forgotten event.

New beginnings really are possible. No web is too tangled, no life too trashed to be redeemed by the gospel of Jesus, both here in this life and for all eternity.

Appendix

FOR PASTORS AND
OTHER LEADERS

Can Regular Churches Do This?

The vision of this book may be inspiring but also puzzling to some pastors and other church leaders. You may be wondering, *How would something like this work in my situation?* You're probably not going to go out and buy a strip club, as happened in Fort Collins. What would it look like, in your settled, established, already-busy congregation, to affect the lives of damaged people in any meaningful way?

Nearly every church across the land has in its creed some version of "We believe in reaching the lost for Christ." That is easy to write, to post on a website, to frame and put up on a wall. The challenge, of course, is moving from orthodoxy to orthopraxy, from creed to deed.

Your first thought may be to outsource this ministry by writing checks to the local rescue mission, the Salvation Army, the pregnancy center, the rehabilitation farm (or even the Genesis Project!). Nothing wrong with that. In fact, each of these entities scrambles constantly to keep the doors open, because the populations they serve are hardly schooled in the Christian discipline of tithing. Budgets are always tight, and every financial gift is an answer to prayer.

But what if you aspire to go deeper, to get corporately and personally involved in, as Isaiah put it, bringing "good news to the poor" and "bind[ing] up the brokenhearted"?[1]

Saturday Mornings and Beyond

Periodic outreaches are common in many churches—providing breakfast or lunch in the city park, doing a clothes-and-shoes giveaway, putting together backpacks full of school supplies for needy children in August, building a ramp for a disabled person's front entrance.

These might be called "excursions into brokenness." They're not bad in and of themselves; at least they put cracks in the wall of self-centeredness. They let church members spend a few hours being generous, after which they can go back to their comfortable surroundings in time to watch the football game.

Such outreaches do run the risk, however, of encouraging a paternalistic instinct: *I've got the resources, and you need my help.* Handouts of various kinds may quiet hungry stomachs momentarily, but they can also demean the recipients if the givers come off as superior.

Plus, there's always the chance that the aid being given isn't actually what the person needs or wants. Deeper than any physical provision is the universal human desire to preserve dignity. In fact, Steve Corbett and Dr. Brian Fikkert have written a powerful book on this entitled *When Helping Hurts: How to Alleviate Poverty Without Hurting the Poor . . . and Yourself*, published by Moody. We highly recommend it.

Full ministry requires going beyond occasional events to building real, authentic *relationships* (there's that word again). It means sitting down and saying, "I'd really like to hear your story." It means going with a heart as much to learn as to teach or help, not assuming that we can quickly fix what's broken in the person or family. Instead, we're willing to *embed* ourselves in their reality.

It means taking Romans 12:16 seriously, which says, "Do not be proud, but be willing to associate with people of low position. Do not be conceited."

Leading the Way

This may not come naturally to pastors if they view themselves at the top of a church hierarchy. Early in my career as a young staff member at a large church, I (Matt) was told by my lead pastor, "Our flock needs a pastor, not a friend." He clearly meant that we, the clergy, should never become too vulnerable or "real" with the congregation. We had to maintain a pastoral persona. Otherwise, lay leaders might pounce on any weakness and make life difficult for us.

Church leaders desperately need to tear down this confessional-booth mentality and start engaging one another face-to-face, as we truly are. Real relationships are never one-way streets. They involve two people being honest with each other, hearing what's really going on inside, and not reacting with condemnation or disdain. Broken people, especially, have already had a boatload of judgment in life. They need us to listen uncritically, to care, and to love.

Churches love to describe themselves with the term *family*: "We're a big family around here." That's easier said than practiced. Family life in a congregation (*koinonia*, to use the common New Testament Greek word) means actually knowing one another and becoming embedded in each other's lives.

> **Broken people, especially, have already had a boatload of judgment in life. They need us to listen uncritically, to care, and to love.**

This is one reason for the coffee shops that every Genesis Project runs, not just on Sunday mornings but throughout the week as well. They certainly don't exist to make money. They exist to create an environment where all of us can just be together and "do life"—the good, the bad, and the ugly.

In some ways they are as important as Sunday morning services. Community is not furthered by sitting in a row and staring at the back of someone's head for an hour. Nice, polished, eloquent words can flow from the podium/platform/stage/chancel, but by themselves they won't get the job done. Redemptive work happens through engagement, involvement, and open sharing of how we're struggling (yes, even we pastors), how we're upset with God at times, how we've failed and have to get back up again.

Look at how God built a relationship with Adam and Eve back at the beginning of time. He didn't call them into a special sanctuary or temple. He exerted himself to come down and simply walk with them "in the garden in the cool of the day."[2] We might even say they "hung out together."

Many, many people today are sick and tired of being anonymous, unknown, disconnected. A fair number never had a dad (or even a mom) who listened to them or earned their respect. They crave healthy relationships. And yes, this kind of engagement takes time. It can get messy. As pastors, the two of us can't engage with nearly as many broken people as we wish—there simply aren't enough hours in the week. But we have to be intentional with at least a handful. We have to show the way. Otherwise, nobody in the congregation who's watching us is going to take this seriously.

Following the Leader

Before long, some church members will catch the vision and want to do likewise. Not everyone, to be sure. Some longtime "pillars" in the congregation may be alarmed at the prospect of their beloved church actually touching those with drug issues or whatever.

But some will warm to the idea of building new relationships. Maybe only five or ten in the beginning. That's all right. Pastors don't have to mobilize the whole infantry (membership) to invade the darkness. A special-ops team is good enough for starters, with the pastor as its captain. Together they start praying and looking for ways to connect with people in need of Jesus.

You will no doubt make mistakes in the early going. We certainly did. The first day my friend Brett and I (Rob) showed up at a low-end motel just outside the city limits, where people live hand to mouth for weeks or even months at a time, we said to the manager, "Um, we're from the Genesis Project, where we like to find ways to serve our community. We just wondered if there was a way we could serve you and your patrons. Like, we could pull weeds. We could put on a barbecue for all the families—"

"Absolutely not!" the man snapped at us. "You start bringing food in here, and the word will travel. I'll have every homeless person in Fort Collins showing up here in my parking lot!"

Oh.

Just then a woman and her adult son walked past the door.

"You want to help people, you say?" the manager barked. "How 'bout you help *her*? She has to go out and panhandle every day to get enough money to stay in this motel. You want to help?" He was calling our bluff.

"Okay," I said. "We'll give it a try." We went back outside, took a deep breath, and started talking to a short woman with salt-and-pepper hair in her late fifties. We asked for her story. We learned that she, her husband, and their son had been displaced way back in 2005 by Hurricane Katrina. They had come to Colorado because somebody said our state had better services for the needy. Later on, they had returned to Louisiana, but then the Baton Rouge floods of 2016 drove them out again. Here they were in Colorado a second time. But they knew they could never afford a place in our expensive city.

As she poured out her story, her extremely shy son said not a word. She added that her husband was out panhandling just then, also, to try to get enough money for them to buy another night's lodging. I knew in that moment what I had to do.

"Just a minute," I said, and walked back inside.

Soon I was back with a room key in my hand. "We care about you, and we just paid for another week here for you guys," I said. "Not that we could keep doing this, but for now, we want to help." The woman burst into tears.

"Maybe we can help your son try to find a job," I added. We exchanged contact information and then left.

Following this, we sent in our "secret weapon"—Martha Crider, the sweetest grandma in the world (whom we introduced back in chapter 3). She absolutely stole the hearts of the manager and his wife. A couple of months later, when we were getting ready to do our annual Wanna Give Away event, we asked him to choose five families who he knew were in desperate need, struggling to support themselves.

Then came the day we parked ourselves in the lobby while he went to the five rooms saying, "There are some people here who can maybe help you." He actually escorted them, one by one, down to see us. We sat down with each of them for thirty to forty-five minutes, just hearing their stories and figuring out ways to help, either through the church or by connecting them with one of the many agencies in town.

The Louisiana family started coming to church. We helped them get back to relatives in Baton Rouge, in fact, which was their best option.

The manager of that motel has come around 180 degrees from his first display of rudeness. We have an open welcome now any time we show up there.

An important point, however: this was *not* done with the goal of getting people into our church. Some people with whom we journey for a long time have never shown up, at least not yet. And the crazy thing is, if you asked them, they would say I'm their pastor and the Genesis Project is their church. Yet they never come.

That's all right. They are feeling the relentless love of Jesus and his people.

If a church member says to you, "I don't know where I would

find needy people in my world—I'm just not around them," well, do something as simple as hanging out at a Laundromat. Who uses a Laundromat? People who don't have their own washers and dryers. Often, these are people in need.

We have members who will deliberately show up with a sack full of quarters and a stack of board games to play with the kids who are otherwise running around raising a ruckus. Soon they're talking with the moms as they push wet loads into the dryers. All kinds of stories come pouring out.

When we host homeless families for a week in our building as part of the FFH program (see chapter 3), we *never* say to our people, "Please come help the poor." We say instead, "This coming week, we get to make new friends!" And, in fact, some of those families end up being our dearest friends.

Relationships have to be organic, like a vine. What a church leader does is build lattices for these vines to climb. Yes, sometimes they grow wild and free; sometimes they grow into areas you'd rather they didn't. But they are *alive*. Jesus isn't afraid of them, and neither should we be.

In fact, the more we share what's happening, the more church people catch the vision. As every pastor knows, we foster what we celebrate in church environments. Let's say a man stands up on Sunday morning and says, "I wasn't so sure about going out and just starting up a conversation with a homeless guy. I guess I'd always assumed those people were lazy and just needed to get a job. Then I met Jake. He told me what all he's been through. I found out what his family did to him in

> Relationships have to be organic, like a vine. What a church leader does is build lattices for these vines to climb.

the early years. He told me how his finances got wiped out, and how hard it is to get restarted now. To be honest with you, I don't know that I could have done any better under the circumstances.

"So we started talking about the fact that Jesus never leaves or forsakes us. He had a lot of questions, and I tried to answer them as best I could. I want to stay in contact with Jake. He's become my friend."

The rest of the congregation listens to this and starts to get inspired. Every new window into this kind of ministry prompts more people to be willing to give it a try.

Special Moments

Soon the special-ops team will grow large enough that intentional events can be put into motion. Here are just a few we've developed over the years:

A Friday night celebration service. Why Friday nights? Because that's a dangerous hour for many broken people. It's when they've gotten in trouble more than once in the past. Now they can say to themselves, "Instead of going out and getting high tonight, there's a safe place for me to be. I need to go there."

A New Year's Eve event, with everything from worship to snacks to showing a good movie. Again, it's the same logic as on Friday night. It keeps people from doing things they will later regret.

A pre–Mother's Day banquet for single moms. Who gives honor these days to those raising kids without a husband? When the women of our Fort Collins church put this together for a night during the week leading up to Mother's Day, they go all out. The place glitters like the Ritz-Carlton. They set up a photo booth where single moms can have pictures taken with their kids, for free. The smiles all around are priceless.

A Thanksgiving dinner but not in the usual *charity* **format.** On the Wednesday before Thanksgiving, we at the Genesis Project–Ogden buy the groceries, get volunteers to cook a great meal, and recruit a church couple or family to host each round table. They are asked to bring their best place settings and centerpieces; some even show up with candles.

On this night hundreds of people arrive. They aren't herded through a serving line like at a soup kitchen. Instead, the host brings the food to the table, and dishes are passed around. Each host has been coached ahead of time to ask icebreaker questions: "So where are you from?" "How long have you been in Ogden?" "What's happening in your life these days?" Stories unfold, and relationships get seeded. Guests say they've never been to such a wonderful dinner in their lives.

A family Christmas festival. Our Fort Collins building isn't large enough to accommodate a sit-down meal, so we do finger foods at stations all around while we talk to people. Despite being located in a dimly lit, industrial part of the city, swarms of marginalized people show up with their kids. They absolutely love it. Our people use every moment to welcome them and build relationships with them. A lot of walls come down in just a few hours.

Santa Claus is there for the kids, and we also have a photographer on hand. We hire a fellow with a horse-drawn carriage to give rides all through the evening so families can huddle under a blanket, sip hot chocolate, and tour around the neighborhood.

How Do We Measure?

In all of these things it is important to focus on the right metrics. What constitutes a win? It is *not* the number of meals served, the number of jackets handed out, the number of backpacks given away. These statistics are easy to tabulate, but they don't align with our goal, which is the transformation of lives.

Maybe the right measurement needs to be how many stories we bring back to the floor of intercession. Suppose somebody says, "I was at the park, and I met Diane, who has two little kids. You won't believe what happened. One of the kids fell and broke her arm, and it was the hospital bills that ended up making them homeless. Now they're on the street, and she's desperately trying to make ends meet."

Suddenly this woman is no longer the recipient of burrito number 113 that was handed out. She's Diane. We start to pray in earnest about her predicament, asking God for wisdom in how to help her and her children.

Leaders have to set expectations for the right metrics, in line with our true calling.

For years in Ogden we used to operate a food bank. Strangers would line up around the block for handouts. We finally shut it down, because we couldn't figure out a way to build relationships with people that would lead to meeting their greatest need: the gospel. Other nonprofits in the community can supply beans and rice and cheese, and in fact, they do it efficiently. Meanwhile, we keep seeking to do what God has called us to do.

People Matter More Than Buildings

Some pastors may say that their churches' very architecture—nice brick buildings on a well-manicured street—is off-putting to people in distress. Can a church accomplish anything being located on the nice side of town?

This does not have to be a barrier unless we allow it to be. I (Matt) was visiting one church building where it seemed like everywhere I turned, there was a sign:

> No FOOD OR DRINK IN THE SANCTUARY!
> Do NOT TURN THIS THERMOSTAT BELOW 72 DEGREES!
> ONLY STAFF AND PARENTS ALLOWED IN THIS AREA!

And this wasn't even the most magnificent church building I'd ever seen.

I said to the pastor, who had invited me to come as a consultant, "You know, when my family and I go to somebody's home for an evening and there are warning signs, 'Take your shoes off,' 'Be careful with this heirloom couch,' or whatever, I get nervous. I'm, like, *I hope I don't break something.* I immediately start worrying about my kids' behavior.

"Is this really the message you want to send to people entering your church?" He readily agreed it was not.

This doesn't mean we shouldn't be good stewards of our church buildings. But it does mean we need to examine

> **Can a church accomplish anything being located on the nice side of town? This does not have to be a barrier unless we allow it to be.**

our values. Are we going to communicate "We value our building" or "We value *you!*"?

If having homeless people sitting on our nicely upholstered pews and treading our carpeted aisles means higher cleaning bills from time to time, so be it.

There's a wonderful account from back in the third century that applies here. In AD 258, the Roman emperor Valerian launched a new crackdown on the Christians in Rome. He issued an edict that all bishops, priests, and deacons should be put to death, and he gave his treasury the authority to confiscate any and all money and possessions from the Christians.

Hearing this, Pope Sixtus II quickly put a young Spanish theologian named Lawrence in charge of the church's funds, which included benevolence for the poor. The pope knew his days were numbered, so he felt Lawrence could maybe do better at managing the church's treasure.

On August 6 of that year, the pope was indeed captured while conducting mass and promptly beheaded.

Lawrence was then ordered to turn over the church's riches. The emperor gave him three days to round up the assets.

> **If having homeless people sitting on our nicely upholstered pews and treading our carpeted aisles means higher cleaning bills from time to time, so be it.**

What did Lawrence do? He quickly sold everything he could, passing the money out to widows and the sick. On the third day, when summoned to the palace, he entered the throne room . . . but then stopped. Gesturing back toward the door, he motioned for a crowd of poor, crippled, blind, and suffering people to stream in behind him. "Here, Your Majesty," he boldly announced, "are the true treasures of the church!"

Emperor Valerian, of course, was not amused. He ordered that Lawrence be grilled on a rack above a crackling fire that very day. (Even there, it is said, the man's spunk did not leave him. While being barbecued alive, he said to his executioners, "I'm well done. Turn me over!")[3]

People are more valuable than bank accounts or buildings. And broken people just want to be embraced and loved. If they can find a place that will openheartedly accept them with all their shortcomings, it doesn't matter if the windows are stained glass or not.

But Is It Safe?

You might ask, "Is it safe to do church this way?" The honest answer: not always. Middle-class "church shoppers" remind us of this fact regularly. Something just feels a little edgy to them in the presence of needy people. They squirm, for example, at being around big guys with tattoos wearing muscle shirts.

But the voice of the Holy Spirit calls us to forsake the safety of the Christian cul-de-sac and bravely run toward the darkest corners of our communities with a message of hope. They're called "dark" for a reason. We will never be able to avoid that.

When the Ogden church, needing more space, moved a few years ago from a good-looking commercial area in one part of town to a larger building in a lower-socioeconomic area, some people said, "Why are we doing this? We're leaving a desirable neighborhood for a neighborhood we personally wouldn't want to live in." Yes, but this was where the greater need awaited.

Of course we take reasonable precautions: we have security teams; we do check-in and check-out procedures in our children's ministry so as not to get caught in custody arguments between estranged parents. But we can never forestall every awkward situation, every danger. We can't sanitize every interaction.

Look what happened to Jesus at the end of his ministry. He did not retire as an old man, going to speak at conferences as a beloved elder statesman. He ended up getting stripped naked and hung on a cross. Have we forgotten what happened to untold thousands of his faithful followers? Have we forgotten how thick the classic *Foxe's Book of Martyrs* is? (It's more than four hundred pages, and covers only three centuries.)

The boldness of Jesus can put us back on our heels sometimes, but it is intrinsic to who he is. Perhaps you remember that wonderful scene in C. S. Lewis's *The Lion, the Witch and the Wardrobe* in which the young sisters are apprehensive about the nature of Aslan (the story's Christ figure). Mr. Beaver says:

> "I tell you he is the King of the wood and the son of the great Emperor-Beyond-the-Sea. Don't you know who is the King of Beasts? Aslan is a lion—*the* Lion, the great Lion."
>
> "Ohh!" said Susan, "I'd thought he was a man. Is he—quite safe? I shall feel rather nervous about meeting a lion."
>
> "That you will, dearie, and no mistake," said Mrs. Beaver, "if there is anyone who can appear before Aslan without their knees knocking, they're either braver than most or else just silly."
>
> "Then he isn't safe?" said Lucy.
>
> "Safe?" said Mr. Beaver. "Don't you hear what Mrs. Beaver

tells you? Who said anything about safe? 'Course he isn't safe. But he's good. He's the King, I tell you."[4]

Jesus did not call us to be safe; he called us to be dangerous. Dangerous to the powers of darkness that guard strongholds in people's lives.

Not Much Competition

A corollary of this fact is that not every group of Christians will want to take up this ministry. As we say when we unpack the story of Mephibosheth and King David (see chapter 7), "There are no traffic jams on the road to Lo Debar." Not many others are headed that way to seek out the crippled person whom society prefers to ignore. The lanes are wide open.

And there is seldom any glory in doing this work. Notice that 2 Samuel 9 doesn't even tell us the names of the servants who found Mephibosheth and brought him to the king's palace. They remain anonymous. They didn't get royal medals for taking on this expedition. They were simply bit players in the larger drama.

Heading out into the world of brokenness today can be a long, lonely journey. It doesn't fit a culture that likes quick fixes, return on investment, and glamorous accolades. We can feel unnoticed, unheralded, unappreciated.

Still, remember the Jesus perspective: "When he saw the crowds, he had compassion on them, because they were harassed and helpless, like sheep without a shepherd. Then he said to his disciples, 'The harvest is plentiful but the workers are few. Ask the

Lord of the harvest, therefore, to send out workers into his harvest field.'"[5]

Some of those workers go to far-flung nations on other continents. Others get deployed to dusty, out-of-the-way Lo Debars here in the homeland. And the Lord of the Harvest smiles, even if few others notice.

Not Smart Strategy

Leaders committed to building a large church quickly may not be excited about ministry to the broken. If you've consciously or even unconsciously bought into the consumerist mentality that says people are basically customers—find out what they want and then give it to them—you won't want to upset the customer base. You're aware they want to be around people like themselves, fellow members of the same demographic. You've no doubt read books by high-profile authors and gone to seminars led by experts who hold up the "homogeneous-group principle" of church growth: birds of a feather flock together, and so forth.

Consumerism doesn't fit very well with reaching the lost, the unattractive, the ones nobody else wants to love. Pastors of established churches who have a heart for this kind of ministry need to pray long and hard about whether they are up for the bumpy road that may lie ahead. This is not for the faint of heart. Leaders will need to develop a thick skin for the e-mails and phone calls from members, especially hefty donors, who would rather not have "that element" sitting next to them in church. (Again, notice the impersonal language—not Randy or Suzanne or Arthur, but "that element.")

Complications Will Never End

Consumerism doesn't fit very well with reaching the lost, the unattractive, the ones nobody else wants to love.

The two of us never get away from the fact that this is hard work. Just when you think everything is under control and the church is running smoothly, surprises jump out of the shadows. Somebody shows up asking for money, and when you start trying to learn their story, they get upset. "Look, I need four hundred dollars *today*! You're a church; you're supposed to be the ones who help people, right?" They're actually offended by the offer of relationship.

The church neither can nor should try to accommodate these serial manipulators claiming to be in a crisis.

We've made mistakes over the years. We've offered to mow a senior citizen's lawn every two weeks through the summer, only to find two healthy teenage grandsons sitting on the front porch watching us work. We've been taken advantage of.

We've learned the hard way not to take people into our personal homes. That can turn dangerous. We have come to say, "The honest truth is, we are not equipped to solve your homelessness today. But we really believe we can help you turn your life around over the course of the next couple of months, if you want us to walk alongside you."

(Exception to this policy: if the person has children in tow, and the overnight temperature is headed for fifteen below, then yes—we're going to get them into a motel.)

When it comes to requests for money, we've learned to copy the response of Peter to the beggar at the Beautiful Gate: "Silver and gold I do not have" (well, not very much, anyway), "but what I do have I give you. In the name of Jesus Christ."[6] The change this kind of person needs is not primarily financial. It is spiritual. Our version of this says, "We don't have very many resources, but we do have people who will love you and journey with you."

Yes, we've helped sincere people move out of a cheap motel into permanent housing. We've paid the first and last month's rent, for example. More often, we've picked up the phone and tapped into other helping agencies in town with deeper pockets.

Sometimes the complication can pop up right in the middle of a Sunday morning. I (Rob) remember one homeless guy in his late twenties who used to come hang out in our coffee shop for hours on end. We would talk with him and try to advance a relationship.

Then one Sunday morning he arrived strung out on some drug; I don't even know which one. Suddenly he was reaching into the tip jar at the coffee bar and grabbing all the cash. Mark Orphan, our associate pastor, saw him and said, "Hey, man—you're going to have to put that back. I mean, if you need help with something, tell me about it, and we'll see what we can do. But that money in your hand needs to go back in the jar."

He got belligerent. I ended up nudging him outside the building, quietly repeating what Mark had said. He tightened up his muscles, got within two feet of my face, and I honestly thought he was about to take a swing at me with his fist.

"Hold on, man," I said. "You know we love you and care about you here. We always have. We've helped you however we could. But right now, you need to leave. Come back when you're sober, and we can have a conversation."

He walked away. I went back inside to start the morning service. I was into my sermon that day when I glanced out toward the coffee shop—and there he was again, more agitated than ever. Mark was trying once again to handle the situation, when all of a sudden, I saw Mark's body go flying backward. The guy had pushed him, almost knocking him to the ground.

We ended up having to call the sheriff's department, which came out and told him in no uncertain terms he'd better move along, or he'd be charged with trespassing. Fortunately he at last got the message. Unfortunately he never did take up my offer to come back in a sober state and continue talking.

So it goes in ministering to troubled souls. It's never going to be a cakewalk. But on the other hand . . .

This Is Dead-Serious Work

The vast majority of broken people who come our way know their brokenness all too well. They are far past trying to hide it. Disaster and death seem not that far away. They just wonder if somebody—anybody, please!—will care.

I (Matt) will never forget the day I was grabbing lunch with our executive pastor, Kyle Hill, at an IHOP restaurant. I looked across the room and saw a guy with a background of addiction who had been coming to our church. I had not talked very long with him—maybe an hour total over the weeks.

He walked up to our table all excited. "Hey, come over here and meet my mom!" he said. "It's my birthday, and we're here celebrating together."

"Sure!" I replied, standing up. "Happy birthday!"

When we got to their table, here is what he said: "Mom, this is Matt from church. And man, *he's just my best friend*."

It was all I could do in that moment to keep from breaking down. What had I done to deserve such a high place in his mind? Very little. I held my composure, but I had lost my appetite. I left Kyle and went out to sit in the car, weeping.

Somehow or another in my preaching and informal conversation, I had implied a promise to this lonely young man that I knew I wasn't keeping. The Holy Spirit seemed to say to me in that car, *This isn't a game, Matt. He honestly views you as his lifeline. You can count him as a number in your church and feel good about having a growing crowd on Sundays. But for that young man, this is dead serious.*

To this day, it breaks my heart to remember that day at IHOP. I had somehow overpromised and was underdelivering.

I meet with him now as I'm able. His battle with drugs is not yet won, but he's making progress. Other people in the church are stepping up to supplement what I'm trying to grow within him, which is divine power to set him entirely free.

Jesus made a shocking statement when he described the hungry, the thirsty, the homeless, the unclothed, the sick, the imprisoned. He said, "Truly I tell you, whatever you did for one of the least of these brothers and sisters of mine, you did for me."[7]

The two of us have to say, we've never encountered Jesus so deeply as when we love a broken, wounded person. To see Jesus in the blotchy face of an opioid abuser or a battered woman is a revelation like no other.

Yes, there are highs and lows in this work, thrills and disappointments, victories and relapses. Sometimes we feel like we know less than we ever have. It's the hardest we've ever worked in all our years in the ministry. But we wouldn't trade it for a half-million-dollar salary at the largest church in America.

It is incredibly stretching and invigorating to put oneself in a place where, apart from the power and presence of Jesus, there really is no hope. He truly is the answer for this broken world.

NOTES

Chapter 1: "Anybody Wanna Buy a Strip Club?"

1. Corrie ten Boom, *The Hiding Place* (1971; Uhrichsville, OH: Barbour, 2000), 211.
2. Romans 1:14, emphasis added.
3. Romans 1:16.

Chapter 2: Immersed in a Messy World

1. The Message.
2. Isaiah 61:1–2.
3. Luke 5:31–32.
4. Luke 19:10.
5. Luke 14:21, 23.
6. Gary A. Haugen, *Just Courage: God's Great Expedition for the Restless Christian* (Downers Grove, IL: InterVarsity, 2008), 31–32.
7. See, for example, the NPR story "Cul-de-Sacs: Suburban Dream or Dead End?" at https://www.npr.org/templates/story/story.php?storyId=5455743.
8. Matthew 5:3.
9. Tim Keller, *Generous Justice: How God's Grace Makes Us Just* (New York: Penguin Books, 2012), 102–103.
10. 1 Corinthians 1:26, 28–29.
11. Isaiah 61:2–4.
12. Matthew 8:3, emphasis added.

13. John 12:26.
14. Paul Borthwick, *Great Commission, Great Compassion* (Downers Grove, IL: InterVarsity, 2015), 47.

Chapter 3: We Pursue Real Relationships
1. John 13:34, 35; 15:12, 17; Romans 12:10; 13:8; Galatians 5:13; Ephesians 4:2; 1 Thessalonians 3:12; 4:9; Hebrews 10:24; 1 Peter 1:22; 3:8; 1 John 3:11, 23; 4:7, 11, 12; 2 John 5.
2. Ezekiel 36:26–27.
3. 1 John 4:19.
4. Acts 3:6.
5. Ruby K. Payne, *A Framework for Understanding Poverty: A Cognitive Approach* (Highlands, TX: aha! Process, 2013), 109–10.
6. Genesis 3:8.
7. Matthew 25:40.

Chapter 4: We Open Up True Stories
1. Romans 6:23.
2. Genesis 50:20.
3. Luke 14:35 and elsewhere.
4. Henry Wadsworth Longfellow, "The Fire of Drift-Wood" (1857) in *The Prose Works of Henry Wadsworth Longfellow*, vol. 3 (Boston: Ticknor and Fields, 1866), 361–62.
5. "None of Us Are Sinners Emeritus: An Interview with Bruce Larson," by Dean Merrill, *Leadership*, Fall 1984, 13–14.
6. James 5:16.
7. See John 16:8–11.
8. 1 Corinthians 11:27 KJV.
9. Luke 15:17.
10. Exodus 33:15.

Chapter 5: We Pull Together Safe Communities
1. Ephesians 4:3, emphasis added.

2. Ephesians 4:3 NLV, emphasis added.

3. Romans 12:16.

Chapter 6: We Get Honest About Sin

1. John 1:17, emphasis added.

2. Deuteronomy 30:15, 19–20.

3. John 14:6.

4. E. Stanley Jones, *The Way* (Minneapolis: Summerside, 2011), xiii.

5. Ibid., 2.

6. Ephesians 4:15.

7. Hebrews 12:2.

8. Jones, *The Way*, 2–3.

9. Henry Cloud, *Necessary Endings* (New York: HarperBusiness, 2011), chap. 7.

10. 1 Corinthians 10:12.

11. John 8:11.

12. Ecclesiastes 1:14, 17; 2:11, 17, 26; 4:4, 6, 16; 6:9.

13. Ecclesiastes 2:10–11.

14. Matthew 19:22.

Chapter 7: We Extend God's Forgiveness and Freedom

1. Ernest Hemingway, "The Capital of the World," first published in *Esquire* magazine (June 1936), and included in a later collection called *The Fifth Column and the First Forty-Nine Stories* (New York: Scribner's, 1938).

2. Galatians 5:1.

3. 2 Samuel 4:4.

4. 2 Samuel 9:7.

5. 1 Timothy 1:16.

6. Luke 15:20–23.

7. Isaiah 43:25.

8. As told on a Richard Dobbins audiocassette titled "The Healing of Memories." Transcribed and reproduced in *The God Who Won't Let Go* by Dean Merrill (Grand Rapids, MI: Zondervan, 1998), 97–98.

9. Mark 2:1–12.

10. Ephesians 2:10 NLT.

11. Galatians 4:9.

12. "Men Met in Hotel Lobbies," *Washington Post*, June 16, 1901, 18.

13. Luke 11:4.

14. Matthew 6:14–15.

15. C. S. Lewis, "On Forgiveness" (1947), included in *The Weight of Glory and Other Addresses*, rev. and exp. ed. (New York: Macmillan, 1980), 125.

Chapter 8: We Help Reset Lives and Habits

1. Galatians 5:16.

2. Galatians 5:16 NLT.

3. See John Ortberg, *Growth: Training vs. Trying* (Grand Rapids, MI: Zondervan, 2000).

4. Galatians 5:25.

5. Philippians 3:13–14.

6. See http://liferecoverygroups.com.

7. Philippians 1:6.

Chapter 9: We Deal with Ongoing Complications

1. Mark 5:1–20.

2. Luke 15:31, emphasis added.

3. "Good Landlord Program," OgdenCity.com, accessed February 26, 2018, https://www.ogdencity.com/203/Good-Landlord-Program.

4. See 2 Corinthians 6:14–16.

5. 1 Corinthians 7:15–16.

Chapter 10: We Don't Give Up When Setbacks Occur

1. 2 Corinthians 7:9–11, 13.

2. Matthew 27:3.

3. Matthew 26:75.

4. John 21:15–17.

5. See Acts 2:14–41.
6. See Acts 3:1–10; 5:15–16; also Acts 9:32–35 and 9:36–42.
7. See Acts 10–11.
8. Jeremiah 31:16–17.

Chapter 11: We Share the Victories
1. Mark 5:19–20.
2. John 4:39.
3. See Luke 19:10.

Chapter 12: It's Simple (but Not Easy)
1. See John 4:43–53.
2. See Luke 7:1–10.
3. See Mark 9:14–27.
4. See Mark 2:1–12.
5. John 15:5.
6. John 6:68.
7. 1 Corinthians 1:26–29.
8. Luke 18:22.
9. Luke 9:23.
10. Luke 5:5, emphasis added.
11. Genesis 2:17.

Chapter 13: The Art of Spiritual Kintsugi
1. See also Amy Azzarito's article "The Most Glamorous Way to Fix a Broken Ceramic," *Architectural Digest*, June 19, 2017, www.architectural digest.com/story/*kintsugi*-japanese-art-ceramic-repair.
2. Isaiah 61:3 NKJV.
3. Isaiah 61:3.

Chapter 14: The Gospel Still Works—Here and Now
1. See Romans 1:15.
2. 1 Timothy 1:13–16, emphasis added.

3. Blaise Pascal, *Pensées* (New York: Penguin, 1966), 75.

4. 1 Corinthians 1:20–21.

5. See Acts 17:1–10.

6. 1 Thessalonians 1:5–7.

7. See John 11:17–44.

8. See Matthew 16:18–19.

9. C. T. Studd, *H.A.M. [Heart of Africa] Magazine*, November 1915, in Norman P. Grubb, *C. T. Studd, Athlete and Pioneer*, 3rd ed. (World-Wide Revival Prayer Movement: Atlantic City, NJ, 1937), 170.

Appendix: For Pastors and Other Leaders

1. Isaiah 61:1.

2. Genesis 3:8.

3. As recorded by Brandon Vogt at "St. Lawrence and the True Treasures of the Church," *Word on Fire* (blog), August 10, 2016, https://www.wordonfire.org/resources/blog/st-lawrence-and-the-true-treasures-of-the-church/4878.

4. C. S. Lewis, *The Lion, the Witch and the Wardrobe*, Collier ed. (New York: Macmillan, 1950), 75–76.

5. Matthew 9:36–38.

6. Acts 3:6.

7. Matthew 25:40.

About the Authors

ROB COWLES is the founding/lead pastor of the Genesis Project in Fort Collins, Colorado. He has served in full-time pastoral ministry since 1988, including roles as senior pastor of Radiant Church (Colorado Springs) and executive pastor of Timberline Church (Fort Collins). He and his wife, Joy, use some of their spare time to carve canyons on their Harley-Davidson motorcycle. They have two grown sons, the younger of whom is a staff member at the Genesis Project in Ogden, Utah.

For more information, go to
www.genesisfortcollins.com.

MATT ROBERTS is the founding/lead pastor of the Genesis Project in Ogden, Utah, a church that has grown from one local site to become a model in multiple cities and towns across the United States. He began his ministry as a youth pastor in the inner cities of Tampa, Florida, and Portland, Oregon. In addition to his present ministry in Utah, Matt has consulted with various churches and denominations seeking to reach dark areas with the hope of Jesus. He and his wife, Candice, are the parents of four sons.

ABOUT THE AUTHORS

For more information, go to
www.genesisutah.com.

DEAN MERRILL is an award-winning author and editor with fifty books to his credit. He and his wife, Grace, live in Colorado Springs.